RETIRE TODAY

Create Your Retirement Master Plan In

5 SIMPLE STEPS

Author Photograph by: Carley Marie Photography
Published by Niche Pressworks; NichePressworks.com
Indianapolis, IN

ISBN
Paperback   978-1-962956-73-4
Hardback   978-1-962956-72-7
eBook   978-1-962956-74-1

Library of Congress Control Number: 2025910589

To protect their privacy, the names, dates, ages, and identifying details of clients have been changed throughout this work.

The views expressed herein are solely those of the author and do not necessarily reflect the views of the publisher.

RETIRE TODAY

Create Your Retirement Master Plan In
5 SIMPLE STEPS

JEREMY KEIL, CFP®, CFA®

Niche Pressworks
Indianapolis, IN

DISCLOSURE

For Educational Purposes Only – Not Investment Advice

The content in *Retire Today* is provided for general educational and informational purposes only. The examples, scenarios, and case studies included in this book are hypothetical and intended to illustrate potential retirement planning considerations. These examples are fictionalized or anonymized and may not represent actual client outcomes or situations.

No Personalized Recommendations or Guarantees

This book does not constitute personalized investment advice, financial planning, tax advice, legal advice, or a recommendation to buy, sell, or hold any security, product, or investment strategy. Readers should not interpret any specific action or outcome described in this book as a guaranteed or advisable strategy for their own situation. Individual circumstances vary, and financial decisions should be made based on an individual's goals, time horizon, risk tolerance, and overall financial condition.

Hypothetical Results & Assumptions

All planning tools, projections, and outcomes discussed in this book are hypothetical in nature and based on a variety of assumptions which may not hold true for your situation. Any forward-looking statements, projections, or "rules of thumb" are not predictive of actual results. Past performance does not guarantee future returns. Investment outcomes are inherently uncertain and may result in gains or losses.

Tax and Legal Disclaimers

The content herein may reference tax strategies (e.g., Roth conversions, Net Unrealized Appreciation rules) or estate planning concepts. Such discussions are general in nature and not intended to provide, nor should they be construed as, tax or legal advice. Readers are strongly encouraged to consult with qualified tax professionals, legal counsel, and other appropriate advisors before acting on any information contained in this book.

Third-Party Content and Tools

Where external tools, calculators, or regulatory references are mentioned (e.g., IRS publications, annuity calculators), those resources are provided for illustrative purposes. The publisher and author do not guarantee the accuracy, timeliness, or applicability of any third-party content or external tool mentioned.

No Fiduciary Relationship

Use of this book or its content does not create a client, advisory, or fiduciary relationship between the reader and Jeremy Keil, Keil Financial Partners, Alongside, LLC, or any of their representatives.

Affiliations and Conflicts of Interest

Keil Financial Partners offers investment advisory services through Alongside, LLC, a registered investment adviser. Any references to specific strategies or planning processes reflect the author's professional perspective but do not necessarily reflect the views of Alongside, LLC. Keil Financial Partners, "Mr. Retirement," and the *Retire Today* book and podcast are not affiliated with Alongside, LLC. The opinions expressed are solely those of the author, hosts, and their guests. The author may benefit commercially from sales of this book or advisory relationships formed as a result of its publication.

Use of this Material

Do not rely solely on the content of this book for making financial decisions. Always consider seeking professional advice tailored to your specific circumstances before implementing any strategies discussed.

For those worried about retirement and wondering,
"How do I actually retire?" — this book is for you.

Contents

Don't Climb Mount Retirement Alone

WE OFTEN TALK about retirement planning in the same way we describe summiting Mount Everest: we know it's possible because other people have done it, but it can be tough to imagine ourselves actually accomplishing it. There are so many important details that can affect your quality of life in retirement, and you don't know what you don't know.

Making the wrong investing move, stumbling into an expensive tax problem, or opting for a disastrous retirement date all seem more likely than the possibility of enjoying a secure and fulfilling retirement. It's no wonder that 61 percent of working Americans[1] are more afraid of retirement than death!

If more of us had a guide to the necessary preparation, mindset, and expectations for retirement, we would be much more likely to look forward to the prospect of climbing Mount Retirement instead of avoiding it.

That's where Jeremy Keil, aka Mr. Retirement, comes in.

Jeremy is the guide you need. This book is the map to your retirement summit. And today is the day you can start the process of retiring when you want to.

In the pages that follow, you'll meet several of Jeremy's clients as he ushers them through the stages of retirement planning using his five-step Retirement Master Plan process. These steps help you plan ahead for spending, income, taxes, and investing in retirement, as well as leaving a legacy.

With guideposts every step of the way, Jeremy helps you to learn, do, and follow the retirement math so you can maximize your retirement income. He helps you identify what you don't know so you can ask the right questions and breaks down the specific information you need to gather to help you answer those questions. And he gives you the confidence you need to follow and trust in your Retirement Master Plan as you get closer to your retirement date.

But Jeremy doesn't just focus on dollars and cents, taxes and investments, spending and saving. He also guides you through the emotional component of retirement. Jeremy knows that money is emotional, and through savvy advice and relatable stories, he will help you navigate the tough emotions that can keep you from the retirement you deserve.

You will learn how to avoid the kind of financial panic that might lead a nervous investor to cash out when the market has hit rock bottom. You will question whether traditional retirement processes, which may feel more secure since it's how everyone does it, will work for you as an individual. And you will recognize how to protect yourself from the "retirement consumption puzzle," which often keeps retirees from spending their hard-earned money in retirement.

Achieving a financially stable and personally enjoyable retirement may seem as unlikely as reaching the top of Mount

Everest — but you don't have to climb the mountain alone. Jeremy Keil is here to help. With his engaging and easy-to-follow guidance, you can create your Retirement Master Plan and enjoy yourself in the process.

Today is the day you start planning your adventure.

— EMILY GUY BIRKEN

Emily Guy Birken is a former educator, lifelong money nerd, and a Plutus Award-winning freelance writer who specializes in the scientific research behind irrational money behaviors. She is the author of *Choose Your Retirement, Making Social Security Work for You, End Financial Stress Now,* and the bestseller, *The Five Years Before You Retire.*

DISCLOSURE:

The views and opinions expressed in this foreword are those of the author and do not constitute an endorsement or testimonial. The author is not a client of Jeremy Keil or Keil Financial Partners, nor has the author received any form of compensation, financial or otherwise, for contributing this foreword. Any statements made are for illustrative or editorial purposes only and should not be interpreted as investment, legal, or tax advice. Readers are encouraged to consult with a qualified financial professional before making any financial decisions.

CHAPTER 1

Retire When You Want To

"I'VE HAD IT!" Mike thinks as he walks out of the airport. Holding his laptop bag in one hand and wheeling his carry-on suitcase with the other, he spots his wife, Lisa, standing next to their car and waving. Sighing as he kisses her cheek, Mike pops the trunk and lifts in his suitcase. Then he turns to Lisa and says, "Can you drive home, honey? I'm just too tired."

They start to drive in silence, until Lisa can't take it anymore. "Rough trip?" she asks. Mike takes a minute, then says, "I'm just sick and tired of all this work travel. If I'm going to pack a suitcase, fly on an airplane, and sleep in a hotel bed, I'd rather be on a vacation or visiting our grandchild, not going on another work trip. I don't know if I can take six more years of this."

Lisa replies, "After your heart attack last year, I hope you'll still be around in six years!"

Now Mike is really fired up. "Who made 65 retirement age anyway? My dad worked his whole life until he was 65, then retired and only got to enjoy retirement for five years before he died. If I want my retirement to last longer than his, I'd better find a way to retire sooner than he did."

Lisa asks, "What's holding you back then? We've been saving our whole life, and the company stock in your 401(k) keeps going higher. I'm sure we could make it work."

Mike says, "I'm not interested in 'making it work.' I just got to a six-figure income, and that will help buy a lot of plane tickets for us to visit the grandkids. Then again, I don't really have the time to visit the grandkids. And how am I going to get health insurance? I'm 59 years old and Medicare doesn't start until I'm 65. I can't go without health insurance for six years! If I had health insurance and I knew we would be OK with money each month, I would retire today if I could."

Lisa says, "I'd love for you to retire today, Mike, but you're right, we need the health insurance, and I don't even know where to begin figuring out if we have enough to retire. Do you think Bill, our insurance agent, can help us out?"

Mike laughs, "I wish. Every time he comes over, he stays too long, drinks too much of our coffee, and only talks about himself. Honestly, I think helping someone retire is above his pay grade."

"You're right," says Lisa as she pulls into the driveway. "I guess you'll just have to keep on working until we can figure out how to actually make retirement work."

"Well, I don't think I can take it anymore," says Mike. "Monday morning, I'm calling in to Bill's manager to ask them for someone else who can help us learn how to retire."

———

Monday morning, I get to the office early, plan out my week, and seeing that I don't have any client appointments until that afternoon, I begin reading my study guide for the CERTIFIED FINANCIAL PLANNER® exam I'll be taking later that month.

Just as I open the book, the office director, Chris, pops in and says, "I've got someone on the phone who needs to switch to an advisor who specializes in retirement planning. You were just telling me about what you learned in the retirement planning section of the CFP® coursework, so I thought of you."

"Thanks, Chris," I say, "I'll see how I can help."

I pick up the phone, "This is Jeremy. How can I help you?"

"Are you the retirement guy?" asks the person on the other end of the phone.

"I suppose you could say that," I reply, "I do spend a lot of time studying financial planning and especially how to retire. What's your name again?"

"My name is Mike. Can you help me and my wife Lisa retire as soon as possible?"

I say, "I'm not sure if you'll be able to retire today, but I've spent a lot of time studying retirement planning, and I think I can help you figure out how to make retirement work."

"That's just what I'm looking for," Mike says. "Can we meet this week?"

"Sure thing!" I say, "How about tomorrow?"

The next day, I drive out to Mike and Lisa's home, turn down their street, filled with older but nicer homes, park in their driveway, ring the doorbell, and am invited to sit down at their dining room table.

"Mike tells me he wants to retire," I say to Lisa, who looks at Mike, smiles, and says, "I'd like him to retire, too. He's a lot more stressed at work, which I don't think is good for his heart, and we just had our first grandchild. I'd love for Mike to retire as soon as possible so we can spend more time with the baby. Mike only has so much vacation time each year."

I say, "That's great! It sounds like you both want Mike to retire. I can't promise that he can retire today, but I can promise we'll figure out if he's able to retire today."

"Sounds great to me," says Mike. "How do we get started?"

I tell them, "You already know that you want to retire, and what you want to do in retirement. Now, we need to find out if and when you can make that happen. I'll start by looking at what you have for investments, income, and insurance options. Here's what you'll need to get:

- Both of your Social Security statements.
- Your latest tax return.
- Your 401(k) statement and something called your "Summary Plan Description," which describes all the rules for your 401(k).
- Your pension info and the Summary Plan Description for that pension.
- Information on your retiree health plan, which might be part of a retirement packet of info the company could share with you."

Summary Plan Description (SPD): A document summarizing the key details of your benefit plan, such as your 401(k) or pension. It outlines important rules, including when and how you can access funds, tax consequences, how you earn pension benefits, and how starting your pension early may affect your payments.

"That sounds like a lot of stuff. Our last advisor never asked for all that," says Mike.

"You're right," I tell them, "It is a lot of stuff. Planning for retirement is like putting a puzzle together, except a lot of times you don't know what the puzzle looks like at the start. You have to find the puzzle pieces, and there is more than one way they can fit together, so you have to figure out which way to put them together that works best for you."

Mike and Lisa promise to start finding the puzzle pieces of their investments, income, and insurance accounts, and I leave their house that night excited to help them find out if they can make retirement work.

The next week, I get an email from Mike: "I've got everything gathered together. Can I drop it off at your office?"

Mike stops by, and as I look at his info, I notice that 85 percent of his 401(k) is in the stock of the company he works for. I ask him if he's aware of that, and Mike says, "I've always worried about having all that money in one stock. I don't want to have all my eggs in one basket, but that's all my employer 401(k) match, and they won't let me move that money to other investments."

I say, "You're in luck then! A law just passed that allows you to diversify out of your employer's stock, and even more important for you, there's another little-known law called Net Unrealized Appreciation that allows you to take the employer stock out of your 401(k) and switch all the gains you have built up from income tax rates over to capital gains tax rates, which are much lower. I'll definitely be looking into this for you."

I look at everything else briefly. It seems to all be in order, and Mike and I set a time to meet again at their house in two weeks.

Net Unrealized Appreciation (NUA): A little-known tax rule that allows you to transfer employer stock from your 401(k), following plan rules, and potentially change the tax treatment of its growth. Instead of paying ordinary income tax on the stock's appreciation, you may qualify for lower long-term capital gains tax rates on the unrealized gains.

Employer stock: Shares of stock in the company where you work. When held within a 401(k), these shares may qualify for Net Unrealized Appreciation (NUA) tax treatment, allowing you to transfer the stock out of the plan under specific rules. This could allow you to pay lower long-term capital gains tax rates on the stock's growth rather than ordinary income tax.

I spend the next two weeks reviewing their tax returns, running projections, and reading the rules of their 401(k) and pension. After learning about all their options and doing all the math related to how their Social Security, pension, and investment accounts could work together, I'm confident I have a plan they can follow.

On the night of our appointment, I drive to Mike and Lisa's house and park the car. As I walk up the sidewalk, Mike opens the door before I get a chance to knock. After we sit down, Mike and Lisa look at each other, then turn to me, and Mike says, "So, when can I retire?"

I pull out my stack of papers and notes and calculations and say, "I've done a lot of research, I've done a lot of math, and I believe you can retire today if you want to."

Mike looks taken aback. "Really? How is that possible? I didn't think I could retire until I was 65 — mainly because that's just what everyone else does."

I say, "Well, the number one reason you can retire today is because you've spent thirty-five years spending less than you make, so you could save and invest each month. The number two reason is that while having 85 percent of your investments in your company stock is incredibly risky, it's been a great stock over the years, and you have a lot more in your 401(k) than you thought you did. And the third reason, which is probably the most important to you, is that since you've worked there so long, I found in your retirement packet that the company will allow you to stay on your current health insurance *and* they'll pay for half the cost of your health insurance between now and when you turn 65."

Mike is speechless, so Lisa takes over and says, "This sounds wonderful, but how do we make it all happen?"

I say, "You're right. Just because you have the ability to retire doesn't mean you should walk into your boss's office and quit immediately. You could retire today, but let's make sure you get the most out of your retirement, and you feel confident in your retirement decisions. Here's what we'll do together:

1. Figure out how much you're likely to **spend** in retirement, which includes the dollar amount that goes into your checking account each month, along with your health insurance costs and your taxes. We also need to project how long you're likely to live in retirement.

2. Maximize how much you'll **make** in retirement by looking at your pension and Social Security, figuring out *when* and *how* to take them so you can get the most money over your lifetime.

3. Try to **keep** more of your money by lowering your lifetime taxes. There are a lot of tax rules, and if you learn those rules, you can make use of the income flexibility you have in retirement to pay taxes when you want to, hopefully at a lower rate than you would have otherwise.

4. Change how you **invest** so that you have the right mix of short-term and long-term investments. You'll need to invest not just for growth, but also for income, and it's not a switch from one to the other; it's finding the right balance that makes sense for you.

5. Prepare for the legacy you will **leave** behind. Some people leave behind some money; some people leave behind some bills. Let's plan for the big risks that could hurt your retirement and plan for how the remainder of your money can go to your kids as easily as possible."

Mike and Lisa are silent, and I can see the gears turning in their heads as they realize they could retire much earlier than they expected and that this process could make it happen.

Mike turns to Lisa and says, "Finally, someone who gets us and who can help us retire early!" Lisa turns to me and says, "What's our next step?"

I say, "The first thing we'll do is call your 401(k) to learn how you can move the company stock out of your 401(k). That will help you take advantage of that special tax rule called Net Unrealized Appreciation, NUA. That will help you save on taxes overall, and it will help you diversify out of one stock into investments that are less risky. I read in the 401(k) Summary Plan Description, the SPD, you could do it, but it doesn't say which forms or what's the procedure. Thankfully, their call center is still open, so we can start right now."

Mike turns to Lisa and says, "Let's do it."

I pull out their 401(k) statement, find the number, and call in. When the person answers, I say, "I'm a financial advisor calling in with Mike about his 401(k) and how he can take out his company stock while still working."

I hand the phone to Mike; he verifies that it's really him calling about his own account, and before he hands the phone back over, he listens to the person at the other end of the call for a few more seconds, and his smile slowly turns into a frown.

I take the phone back, turn on the speakerphone, and I hear from the client service representative, "I'm sorry, but I've never heard of that rule. I wouldn't know where to start."

I calmly say, "That's OK, it's a little-known rule, but the ability to take money from the 401(k) after age 59½ is written on page 10 of your SPD, and the ability to make use of the employer stock tax rule is on page 12."

She responds, "I'm not familiar with the SPD. I just handle the typical questions like moving investments around."

I ask to speak to a manager who might be more familiar with the detailed rules. We wait a few minutes, then hear, "Hi, how can I help you?"

I explain that Mike is past the age of 59½ and that he'd like to make use of both the in-service distribution rule and the Net Unrealized Appreciation rule. Then we hear back, "I don't think he can take money out of the plan while he's still working, and I've never heard of Net Unrealized Appreciation."

In-service distribution: A withdrawal from your 401(k) while still employed. Typically available starting at age 59½, this allows you to roll over funds to an IRA without leaving your job. It could also be used to take advantage of Net Unrealized Appreciation (NUA) rules, potentially lowering taxes on employer stock.

Now I'm beginning to frown, too. "Did I read the info wrong?" I think to myself.

I tell him, "The first rule is on page 10 of your plan rules, and the second rule is on page 12. I think he can do this."

"I'm sorry, but you'll need to speak to our director," he tells us, "And she's not in after 5:00 p.m. You'll have to call back tomorrow."

We hang up the phone, look at each other a little deflated, and agree that we'll call in tomorrow and speak to the director.

The next day, I call Mike at his work number. He picks up and says, "I've been asking a few people at work, and no one has heard of the two rules you're speaking of. I'm not sure we can really do this. How is that going to affect my retirement?"

I tell him, "I'm not surprised. Most employees haven't read their 401(k)'s plan rules, and it seems like from last night, even the people who work in the 401(k) area haven't read their plan rules. Let's talk to the director and see what she has to say."

We call in, talk to a different client service representative and explain the whole situation. Then we're passed to another manager, a different one from last night.

We talk to this manager, explain the whole situation again and ask to speak to the director. He doesn't really want to pass us to the director, since no one usually gets to speak to the director just by calling the 800 number, but when he looks at the plan rules and sees that the two rules we're referring to are listed on the exact same pages we told him about, he realizes we've done our homework! "Let me see if she's available."

We finally get the director on the line, "Hi, it sounds like you have some questions, and it sounds like you know the plan rules pretty well," she says.

Mike explains his frustration, "I've worked here for thirty-five years, and I want to get the most out of my retirement account. My financial advisor found these two rules written in the plan documents, and it seems like no one we talk to at the company knows about those plan rules."

The director says, "I've been here for quite some time, too, and I helped put this document together, so I'm quite familiar with it. I know which two rules you're talking about, but I don't think I've ever had anyone actually ask to make use of those rules. I'm going to have to talk to Legal to figure this out. Mike, you're not going to the retirement seminar the company is holding in two weeks, are you?"

Mike says, "I was planning on it."

The director says, "Great! I'm one of the presenters. I promise to have an answer for you when I see you there in two weeks."

The director hangs up the phone, and Mike and I are still on the line. I say, "I'm sorry this is such a hassle, Mike, but it seems like we found the right person to confirm this for us."

Mike says, "I'm just glad we have you to ask these questions. I would have never known these options were available."

Two weeks later, I get a phone call from Mike. I can tell it's good news from the excitement in his voice.

"Jeremy, I went to the seminar. They told us we get retiree health insurance until 65 and that the company pays for half of it — just like you found in the retirement packet. Then, at the end, the director came up to me and said, 'Mike, I spent the last two weeks calling around and having Legal research our own plan rules. Your advisor is correct. You can roll money out of your 401(k) at 59½, *and* if you follow the rules, you can take that company stock out and make use of that tax rule your advisor found. We couldn't think of any time we had actually done it before, but we see that it's allowed in our rules, and we know exactly the procedure to make it happen. Thanks for telling me about this — I think I'm going to make use of that rule myself!'"

I'm excited; all that research and our persistence with the 401(k) department is about to pay off in Mike retiring six years earlier than he thought he could.

"When do you think you might retire?" I ask Mike.

"Well, before I called you, I called Lisa, and we talked about it. We decided to retire as soon as we could. I walked over to my boss and told him I'd like to retire. He asked if I could finish a project I'm working on for next quarter, and I said I would. I should be retired four months from today!"

"That's great news, Mike," I say, "That gives us four months to make use of those two rules, double-check all the company paperwork, and get you, your investments, and your health insurance all set for the day you retire."

Mike, Lisa, and I meet several times over those four months, filling out paperwork, making sure the tax forms look correct, and moving investments around. Since neither Mike nor Lisa are 62, and there's not even a chance of getting Social Security to start paying their monthly income, we set up their investments to start paying into their checking account each month, starting the first month of retirement.

Everything looks set, but I call Mike and Lisa one week before the official retirement day to see what final questions they might have.

"No questions here," Mike says, "but I do have to tell you what happened last week. I finished the project and gave my report at the quarterly team meeting. Half of them fly in for the meeting, so our tradition is the last day we go out to dinner before they head back home the next day.

"My boss says, 'Mike, since it's your last quarterly team dinner, why don't you have Lisa come along so that we can wish her well on your retirement, too.' I thought that was nice, so I called Lisa and asked her to come along to dinner, too. I went home to pick her up, and we drove out to the restaurant where we always hold our team dinners. But when I talked to the restaurant hostess, she told me we were in one of the private rooms and not at a table like usual.

"We headed over to the private room, and not only were a lot more people there than just my direct team, but both of my kids and their spouses were there! Lisa knew about this all along, so she and my boss surprised me by asking the kids to fly out to what turned out to be my surprise retirement party! It was a great night, Jeremy, and we couldn't have done this retirement thing without you."

"Thanks, Mike, and you too, Lisa, but you were the ones who saved less than you spent the last thirty-five years, and you were the ones who followed the process I put together."

"I suppose you're right," says Mike, "but I never would have retired early if I didn't feel confident in the plan you put together."

———

In the past twenty years since I first met Mike and Lisa, I've met hundreds of people who were in a similar situation. They were closing in on the date they wanted to retire, but they just weren't getting the answers they needed from their co-workers, from HR, even from their financial advisor!

They were scared they couldn't afford retirement. They were overwhelmed because they didn't know where to start. Most of all, they were worried because they "didn't know what they didn't know" — worried that they had spent all this time putting together the perfect retirement spreadsheet, they'd pull the retirement trigger, and then get sideswiped by some financial factor they should have known about, but didn't know how to plan for.

Whether you want to retire today, next year, or five years from now, this book is for you. You'll learn the exact five-step process I take my clients through to create their Retirement Master Plan.

You will learn how to plan for each of these five areas, in the right order, so you can make the best retirement decisions for you. You will learn:

STEP 1: SPEND: How to estimate what you'll be spending in retirement so you can understand if you'll have enough in retirement.

STEP 2: MAKE: How to maximize your lifetime income from your pension and Social Security.

STEP 3: KEEP: How to be proactive with your tax planning so you can lower your lifetime tax bill and keep more of your hard-earned retirement income.

STEP 4: INVEST: How to balance your investments between short-term income and long-term growth so you have money that's ready for you to spend both now and in the future.

STEP 5: LEAVE: How to plan for the big risks in retirement so you don't leave your family with unexpected bills, and how to plan for the money that remains so that your family inherits what you leave them as easily and efficiently as possible.

I spoke to Mike and Lisa just as I finished writing this chapter. They've been retired for over fifteen years. Thankfully, Mike hasn't had any of the health issues he was worried about. Lisa thinks it's because his stress has been way down since leaving work. I think it's because they've been so active. They have visited their two kids, who both live out of state, at least twice every year, and hosted both kids and their families at their house twice every year. They've gone on cruises, European vacations, and road trips and took the whole family to the Grand Canyon.

They've made the most of their retirement and continue to do so, but one thing Mike said in our phone call has really stuck with me, "You know, Jeremy, I never would have retired as soon as I did if you hadn't said, 'Mike, I think you could retire today if you want to,' and then you showed me exactly how to do it."

That's my hope for you with this book. That you learn the process of how to retire so that you become more confident that you and your money are ready to retire, even to the point where you could retire today if you want to.

CHAPTER 2

Plan Your Retirement Today

MOST PEOPLE THINK of retirement in one of two ways. Either it's the time in your life when you can finally do all the things you've always wanted to do, *or* it's the time in your life when you can finally stop doing all the things you don't want to do!

Whichever retirement dreamer you are, whether you are the start-doer or the stop-doer, you know that it's going to take planning — a lot of planning — to make it happen. That's why you read books, watch retirement YouTube videos, listen to podcasts, and create spreadsheets — lots and lots of spreadsheets!

You've never retired before. You don't know what it's like, which is why you want to be prepared for every contingency, every disaster. You don't want to regret your decision to retire, and you want to make sure you and your spouse don't run out of money years down the road when it's too late to unretire.

You're not alone in your focus on the money and the spreadsheets and the what-ifs.

Fritz Gilbert, from the *Retirement Manifesto* blog, interviewed dozens of retirees for advice before he finally retired himself and identified something he calls the 90/10 Rule of Retirement.

"In preparation for retirement, most people spend 90 percent of their planning time on the financial issues and 10 percent on the non-financial issues. After retirement, the ratio reverses, and most retirees spend the vast majority of their time focusing on the non-financial issues of life."[2]

I've seen this type of mindset switch in the hundreds of retirees I've met from over two decades as a financial advisor. Before retirement, there are a lot of worries about having enough money. Then, at retirement, you're worried about whether your money will last now that you're taking it out of your accounts. Finally, there's a peace that you feel after you've made it through a couple of years of living off the money you've saved.

The 90/10 Rule of Retirement seems to be true: the worries and focus on money do seem to drop significantly once you retire, but if you're like me, you're probably wondering, "*Why* is the 90/10 rule true?"

I think you're able to focus on the non-financial parts of retirement in retirement *because* you focused on the financial parts of retirement before retirement.

And I believe the best time to start planning for retirement is today. Not the day you retire, but today — the day you started thinking about the mechanics of retirement planning and started reading this book.

There are two couples I met in the fall of 2019 who stand out in their approach to retirement planning and, so far, their results. One couple wanted to retire and then plan things out; the other wanted to plan things out and then retire.

RETIRE FIRST, THEN PLAN?

Bob and Susan were approaching 65 and wanted to retire the following spring. They were tired of working and curious if they had saved enough to retire. They found my information online, called me up, and booked an evening appointment since they couldn't get off work during the day.

As I sat across the table from Bob and Susan in my office, I asked them, "What makes you want to retire? What would you do?" Bob replied, "I'm just tired of going into the office. I'm sure I'll find something to do."

Susan said, "I just want Bob to be excited about waking up during the week. I think life would be a lot easier if we could go golfing or work in our garden whenever we'd like instead of having to work five days a week and then try to fit in a little fun between all of our chores and errands on the weekend."

I asked them, "You said earlier you'd like to retire on April 1, 2020. What made you choose that date? Do you get a bonus, or is it something to do with health insurance?"

Bob told me, "I don't mind working this next winter since there's not much golf or yard work you can do in Wisconsin in the winter, but I figure once it starts to get nice outside, then that's the perfect time to retire. I'd love for you to figure out if I can make retiring next spring work."

They had brought in all I needed to start putting together their planning — their 401(k) statements, Social Security benefit amounts, and latest tax return. We scheduled a time to meet the following week for them to find out if they could truly retire and what they needed to do to make it happen.

Over the next few days, I researched their 401(k)s, projected their Social Security filing ages, and looked at different ways they could take money out of their accounts to save on taxes over their lifetime.

I put together a plan that I believed would accomplish their goals, and the next week, sitting at that same table, I told Bob and Susan, "I think you can retire, but there are three things you ought to do to make that happen:

1. "Bring the risk down in your 401(k) — you need short-term income investments so you can start to take a monthly payout from your investments when you retire, without having to sell your stock market investments if they happen to be down.

2. "Delay Bob's Social Security — it's the higher benefit of the two, and delaying just the one benefit will help you both in the long run, but it will be especially helpful to whoever is the surviving spouse down the road.

3. "And start doing Roth conversions so you can pay taxes at a lower rate that you choose and hopefully pay less tax overall through the rest of your retirement."

I had put together a great plan with three simple action steps to help them retire when they want and protect them against some of the big risks of retirement: the market going down, living longer than expected, and the heavy burden of taxes.

Bob said, "This is great. I love this plan. We want to start working with you."

I thought the next thing he would say was, "What do we do first?" but instead he continued, "But I don't want to start paying you to be my advisor for the six months before I retire. And the market is hot right now, so I'd like to get my account balances a little higher, too, before I shift some growth money over to short-term investments. I'm retiring April 1, and we can start working together then."

I was stunned. Six months was such a short time away. Their retirement is likely to last thirty years or more. I said, "Why not start planning ahead of time? Let's get your money ready so you can retire when you want, whether the market is up or down on your retirement date."

But Bob was resolute — he liked my planning but wanted to wait six months to start working together. He also insisted that they would definitely be back in touch in six months.

If you've ever worked in the type of job where you talk to potential clients and they say, "Don't call me. I'll call you," you know that really means, "I'll never actually call you."

I fully expected to never hear from Bob and Susan again. And then, in February and March 2020, my attention was quickly drawn toward the constant news about COVID-19 and how it was affecting the world and the financial markets.

That first weekend in March 2020, I received an email from Bob that I wasn't expecting: "I think I need to get on board with you ASAP. Let me know what we need to do."

I was surprised because I didn't think I'd ever hear back from Bob, but it was no surprise what prompted Bob to reach back out: the US stock market had just dropped 12 percent the week before as COVID-19 was starting to bring down the US economy and Bob's dreams of retiring April 1 along with it.

We met on the evening of March 16, 2020. The S&P 500 had just dropped that day by its largest single-day point drop in history. It was now down almost 30 percent for the year.

Bob and Susan looked worried as he said, "I'm sorry I hadn't called you earlier. Now that the market is down so much, I don't think I'll be able to retire for another year, but I do want you to start helping me plan for retirement right away. I realize now I should have started planning for retirement last fall."

We did start working together, making decisions on how to look at the investments now that they were down 30 percent, but Bob and Susan didn't retire even in April 2021 — one year after they originally hoped. The experience of watching the stock market drop 30 percent just before their retirement made them focus even more on the money and having enough before they retired. They didn't retire in April 2021, or April 2022, but finally in April 2024 — four years after they had hoped when we first started talking in the fall of 2019.

PLAN FIRST, THEN RETIRE

In that same fall of 2019, Dave and Kim were also looking to retire soon — hopefully in three more years. They considered themselves to be planners and thought they ought to have a plan in place well ahead of their retirement date.

Unfortunately, every time they asked their current advisor about Social Security, Medicare, and how much they could afford to live on in retirement, they weren't getting the answers they were looking for.

One day, as Dave was driving home through traffic, listening to the *Faith & Finance* radio show, he heard an ad about working with a Certified Kingdom Advisor® financial advisor. Dave got home and told Kim, "We need to see if there are any of those Kingdom financial advisors near us."

They immediately looked online to see who was close by, wrote down a few numbers, and the next day, Dave called me on his lunch break. I say Dave called me because he dialed the phone, but it turned out he had Kim on the line, too!

Dave told me they were not happy with their current financial advisor and asked me a few questions about my background and experience with retirement planning. I answered his questions, then asked them, "What's going on that's making you unhappy with your current advisor?" Kim interjected, "He just doesn't listen to us! We tell him to get more conservative with our money, and I don't think he's doing it."

We booked a time to meet the following week, but before we hung up, I asked, "What would you do if you retired?" Dave said, "We would love to spend three months out of the year in Texas near our son and his family." Kim agreed, "I want to be closer to my grandkids!"

I met Dave and Kim in my office the following week. They shared with me that they wanted to retire in three years, they were worried about the market dropping, and they wanted to make sure they had a plan in place that made the best use of the money they'd saved and the Social Security they'd earned.

Kim said, "I want Dave to retire when we want to retire, and I don't want to have to delay retirement because we didn't get ready ahead of time."

I shared with them how I help people get ready for retirement ahead of time: "Typically, as you approach retirement, I suggest you pull some money away from growth investments toward short-term income investments. That way, you have money to live on in case the market goes down. But you don't move all your money there.

"You also still need money in long-term growth investments to help prepare for your future. Now, some people think you wait until retirement to squeeze every last drop of investment return from your growth investments — but I think that when you're getting close enough to retirement, and especially if the market is near a high point, then you should get ready for retirement and set up your short-term money and long-term money well ahead of time."

Dave said, "That's what we're looking for, a plan we can follow, and I don't think we're getting it from our current advisor. We keep telling him we want less risk, and I don't think he's following our instructions. Just last week, we told him, 'Bring down the risk.' He placed some trades, but I can't tell what he did."

Dave slid a sheet of paper across the table with a list of the trades placed in the account and asked, "Can you tell me if he brought down the risk?"

I looked at the trades, looked up the stock names on my computer, and said, "All he did was sell $12,000 worth of stocks and buy $15,000 worth of stocks, which means he not only didn't bring down the risk, but he took some money out of cash and put it into the stock market."

Then Kim turned to Dave and said, "What are we waiting for? Let's start working with Jeremy."

Over the next month, we refined their retirement planning and decided together that they would:

1. Plan to delay Dave's Social Security so that it could get to its maximum at age 70, which should help them get more income during retirement, especially when the surviving spouse is living on just one Social Security amount.

2. Pull roughly $120,000 from their growth investments into shorter-term income investments so they would have money set aside to live on the first three years of their retirement as they let Dave's Social Security grow.

3. Bring down the risk in their growth investments from 80 percent stock to 60 percent to better match the level of risk they were willing to hold.

Just like Bob sent me an email that was prompted by COVID-19, Dave called me in the first week of March 2020.

I could tell Dave was worried when he skipped his usual questions about how my wife and family were doing. He asked me right away, "At what point do we take all of our money out of the stock market?"

I told him, "Dave, I don't know that I'd ever suggest taking all of your money out of the stock market, especially if you don't need that money for years and years from now. That's why we took some of your long-term growth investments last fall and moved them to shorter-term investments that aren't part of the stock market. Not because we predicted COVID-19 or a stock market drop. It's just that you and Kim wanted to get ready for retirement before you retired, and that was the right move for you."

I looked further into their accounts and told Dave, "Between moving some money toward short-term income investments and bringing down the risk in your long-term growth investments, you moved from roughly 80 percent in the stock market to 40 percent. Your stock risk is half what it was just six months ago!"

Dave's mood started to lighten up, "This is quite a scary time, but you're right. We got ready ahead of time in case something happened, and you told me just what I needed to hear. Let's keep the money that's in the stock market, still in the stock market."

It was our fall 2022 meeting, three years after we first met, when Dave said, "It's official. I'm retiring on December 31. Right on time!" I could feel their excitement as Kim said, "And we've already got our trip planned to visit the grandkids in Texas. We'll be down there for the whole month of January! Thanks for keeping us on track."

THE BEST TIME TO START RETIREMENT PLANNING

Looking back at the fall of 2019, no one could have predicted that COVID-19 would change the world just a few short months later. No one would have expected the stock market to drop 30 percent in just a few months, including a 12 percent one-day drop!

But if you asked me then or ask me today, "When is the best time to start planning for retirement?" I will tell you,

"Today. Whether you want to retire today or retire years from now, the best time to get ready, the best time to set up your investments, is today."

Why start planning for your retirement today? Because when you put in the work today to make sure the financial side of your retirement is set, you'll soon be able to experience what Fritz Gilbert experienced: You'll be able to focus on all the non-financial parts of retirement, the fun parts of retirement, the parts of retirement that don't involve a spreadsheet!

Plan for retirement today so that you can do what you want, when you want, tomorrow.

CHAPTER 3

Do What You Want
When You Want

"I do what I want when I want. I'm retired."

YOU MIGHT HAVE been at a farmers market or a summer festival the first time you saw someone wearing a T-shirt with that phrase. And I bet three things were true about that scene.

1. The person wearing the T-shirt was older than you,
2. They had a big smile on their face, and
3. You can't wait to join them in their world of happy-go-lucky retirement!

The idea of doing what you want when you want summarizes what you're really striving for when you're stuffing money into your 401(k) and dreaming of retirement. You're not dreaming about having all the money in the world — you're dreaming about having all the time in the world!

After meeting with hundreds of people about to retire for over two decades, I haven't quite decided whether it's the "I can do what I want with my time" or the "I don't have to do what others want with my time" that's more appealing.

While the goal of *retiring* is to do what you want when you're *retired*, I find there's a lot of following the same old script in the actual act of retirement. You're planning to "do what you want" in retirement, but when it comes to how and when you retire, you often "do what you think you're supposed to do."

Does this plan sound familiar to you?

Work until you're 65 so that you can get Medicare, start your Social Security and pension ASAP, and then wait until you are 70-plus to start taking the required minimum distributions from your traditional IRA.

Or how about this plan?

Work until you're 59½, when you can take some money out of your 401(k). Take out 4 percent of your balance each year, and try to keep expenses to a minimum until you're 62. Then you can finally start Social Security and get a little extra breathing room in the budget each month, but keep counting down the months until you turn 65 so that you can finally get on Medicare.

It feels like when I ask people, "What's your plan to make retirement work?" they most often give me answers that are based on government-created retirement ages like 59½, 62, 65, or what they've seen others in their company do before them.

COMMON RETIREMENT AGES AND THEIR RELEVANCE

55 If you leave your job at age 55 or older, you can withdraw from that employer's 401(k) without the 10 percent early withdrawal tax penalty (this does not apply to jobs you left prior to 55, even once you are 55).

59½ Withdrawals from your traditional IRA are no longer subject to the 10 percent early withdrawal tax penalty.

62 The earliest age for receiving Social Security retirement benefits.

65 The age at which you become eligible for Medicare.

67 The full retirement age (FRA) for Social Security if you were born in 1960 or later. Claiming benefits at this age provides your full retirement benefit, but delaying until age 70 increases your monthly payment by up to 24 percent.

70 The age when your Social Security benefit reaches its maximum amount — approximately 24 percent higher than if claimed at full retirement age. You do not get any further increases for filing past age 70.

70½ The age when you can begin making qualified charitable distributions (QCDs) — direct donations from your traditional IRA to a charity — without paying taxes on the withdrawal. This was also the previous required minimum distributions (RMDs) start age before recent law changes.

73 & 75 (New RMD Ages):

- If you were born before 1960, you must start taking required minimum distributions (RMD) at age 73.
- If you were born in 1960 or later, your RMD start age is 75.

If everyone else retires at 55 and takes the "Social Security level pension" or waits until 59½ to "get access to their 401k" or retires at 62 and takes the "lump-sum pension option," then that's what they are likely to do.

They want to exercise their freedom in retirement but follow the "how to retire" actions that they feel the government allows them or that the company culture dictates.

Required minimum distributions (RMDs): Mandatory withdrawals from traditional retirement accounts. You will pay a tax penalty if you do not take your RMDs on time.

Social Security level/accelerated pension option: If you retire before age 62, this pension option provides higher monthly payments until age 62, when it is permanently reduced by the estimated amount of your age 62 Social Security benefit. This shifts more pension income to the early years of retirement but results in a lower lifetime pension payment if you live longer than expected.

Because of the drop in guaranteed monthly income at 62 from this option, many retirees feel pressured to claim Social Security early, at up to a 30 percent reduction from their full retirement age amount, even if it is not the best financial decision for them.

This option is more common in government pension plans than corporate pension plans.

AGE 55 VS. 59½ FOR ACCESS TO RETIREMENT ACCOUNTS

Most people are familiar with age 59½ as the age when they can withdraw from IRAs without a 10 percent early withdrawal tax penalty. However, many mistakenly believe this is also the rule for 401(k) plans, leading them to target 59½ as their retirement age so they can avoid the 10 percent penalty with their 401(k).

In reality, the 401(k) withdrawal age is 55. If you retire in or after the year you turn 55, you can access the 401(k) from that employer without penalty. This is often surprising, as the 59½ rule is widely known. However, you can confirm it in IRS Publication 575, Pension and Annuity Income.

If you're considering retirement at 59½ for 401(k) access, you may have more flexibility than you think, starting four-and-a-half years earlier!

Lump-sum pension option: An option to receive a one-time payment from your pension instead of guaranteed lifetime monthly payments. Pensions typically provide guaranteed monthly income starting at your normal retirement age, but many plans allow you to take a lump sum instead.

The lump-sum amount is calculated by plan actuaries based on interest rates and life expectancy, which means the value is not based on a formula like your normal retirement age pension amount but instead fluctuates up and down based on economic conditions.

Just like you want to do what you want when you want in retirement, I'd encourage you to do what you want when you want with the actual act of retiring.

Absolutely, learn the math and the rules related to tax consequences, Social Security, health insurance, and pensions, but more often than not, I've found that the ideas and reasons shared with me about when people want to retire and how to use their money to retire is more based on hearsay and tradition than facts and research.

That's why I like to share two rules when you're planning for retirement.

RETIRE TODAY RULE #1

Retire when you want to and can afford to, but start your pension, Social Security, and 401(k) when it gives you the most money over your lifetime.

(And chances are, those are all different start dates.)

RETIRE TODAY RULE #2

Learn the math, do the math, and follow the math.

(And chances are, your co-workers, friends, and relatives who are giving you their opinion on what to do didn't bother to do the first part of learning the math, let alone all three parts!)

And while I put the "Learn the math" rule after the "Retire when you want to" rule, I think that learning the math, doing the math, and following the math for your particular retirement situation is what will allow you to retire when you want to and can afford to.

I was at my desk late in the year when my fellow advisor John knocked on my office door and said, "Someone's on hold. He said he's a friend of our client Karen, and he *has to* talk to you about retirement."

I picked up the phone and asked, "How can I help?" They responded:

"My name is Jeff. I'm an engineer, and I want to retire next year so my wife, Michelle, and I can travel more. My co-worker Karen told me you're helping her with retirement, and you recommended she do two things I've never heard anyone recommend before.

"First, you told her she's better off taking the monthly life-time pension payments instead of the one-time lump-sum option. Second, you told her she's better off delaying her pension and starting it two years after she retires!

"Every other person I know who has retired, and every other financial advisor I've talked to says, 'Take the lump-sum option right away and invest it,' and you said to do the complete opposite. You said to take the monthly lifetime payments and start them two years later. I've got to know why!"

I replied, "Sure thing! I just did what I always do. I looked at your company's pension calculator site, learned all of the different options, put the info into a spreadsheet, and calculated which one has the best present value. Then I suggested she take the option that gave her the best chance at the most money over her lifetime."

Present value: The amount of money needed today to produce a series of future cash flows based on current interest rates and a specific time frame.

In pensions, an exact length of time is not used, but is instead determined by the probability of a retiree living long enough to receive each future payment, using mortality tables to estimate life expectancy.

Jeff said, "That's what I heard — and I want to meet you and your magical spreadsheet!"

I told him, "There's nothing magical about the spreadsheet. It's just learning the math, doing the math, and following the math. Unfortunately, I've found most people don't even bother with that first step."

"You're right!" Jeff said, "I've been trying to figure out the math behind retirement, and instead, I've found that everyone has an opinion with nothing to back it up!"

Jeff and I met the next week over Zoom, and I asked him to log into his pension calculator site and share his screen so we could find all his different pension options.

Jeff had the same remark as virtually everyone else I've ever met with a pension: "I've already done this, so I'm not sure you're going to find anything different. I already have my two options saved — retire this year and start my pension right away and retire next year and then start my pension."

I said, "That's great. You're definitely looking at different options, and that helps with retirement planning for sure. However, you're making the same assumptions I see virtually everyone else make. You're assuming that the only option you have to grow your pension is to keep working and that you have to start your pension right away.

"You do, most of the time, get credit for working another year. But sometimes you don't. And I'm also curious how much credit you get. When I look at pension projections, I like to isolate the 'working credit' part of it and see how much extra pension you earn by working another year.

"You also, most of the time, get credit for getting older. I call it 'age credits.' You often get a higher pension just by having a birthday. I want to tell the calculator that you will retire at a specific age but then keep asking it to wait to start your pension for one year, two years, even three or more years, however long the calculator will let us project. That way, we can see how much you get in age credits by waiting to start your pension.

"Sometimes I've seen huge age credits, where the pension grows 16 percent every year you wait. Sometimes they are small, perhaps only 2–3 percent, and I've even seen it where you get zero credit or even start losing money because you waited to start your pension.

"You don't know until you take a look, and it'll take me about ten minutes to help you get all your working credit and age credit info. That way, you can make a well-informed decision on your pension."

WHY YOU NEED TO SEPARATE YOUR
PENSION'S WORKING CREDITS AND AGE CREDITS

When calculating a pension, two factors typically increase your benefits:

1. Working Credits: Gained by continuing to work, often increasing your pension.
2. Age Credits: Earned by delaying the start of your pension, sometimes leading to a higher payout.

Many people look at their pension estimates and see an increase, but they don't know whether it's from working longer or simply getting older — and they don't realize that there's a difference. When you can understand how each factor increases your pension (or not), it will help you make better decisions about how long to work and when to start your pension.

WHY THIS MATTERS

- Some people believe, "I have to keep working to grow my pension," when in reality, their pension is frozen, and they're only getting age credits or perhaps no increases at all.
- Others don't realize that working just a few more months after already working twenty, twenty-five, or thirty years could significantly boost their pension.
- Some people are waiting to start their pension but are getting no additional growth and are missing out on hard-earned pension money.
- Others start their pension as soon as they can, not realizing they could increase their payout by 16 percent just by waiting another year.

You truly don't know how your pension works and how to get the most out of your pension until you look at how your additional work and increase in age affect your pension.

HOW TO CALCULATE YOUR AGE AND WORKING CREDITS SEPARATELY

Age Credits

To isolate age credits, assume you stop working today but delay your pension start date by one, two, or more years. This will show how much waiting alone increases your pension (or doesn't).

Working Credits

To isolate working credits, assume you continue working for one, two, or more years. Since these estimates also factor in getting older, subtract the pension increase from your age credit estimates to determine the growth from your working credits alone.

We pulled info on all Jeff's different pension options, first making assumptions about working one to two additional years, then we made the assumption that he retired at a specific year, but waited for one, two, three-plus years before starting his pension.

Then we pulled info on three payout methods: the promised pension, called single life annuity (SLA); the pension that pays out the same to Michelle if Jeff is no longer living, called 100 percent joint and survivor annuity (JT100); and the lump-sum option value.

Finally, we put the numbers into my "magical spreadsheet" to calculate how much the different parts of the pension grew each year.

Age	SLA	JT100	JT100/ SLA	Lump Sum	SLA Growth	JT100 Growth	Lump Growth
60	$4,334	$3,692	85%	$547,439			
61	$4,667	$3,985	85%	$581,746	7.7%	7.9%	6.3%
62	$5,000	$4,278	86%	$616,053	7.1%	7.3%	5.9%

We could see how the joint 100 percent survivorship option paid about 15 percent less than the single life annuity option, which met my expectations. We could see how the monthly lifetime income options were guaranteed to grow from 60 to 61 to 62 and how the lump-sum option was projected to grow each year.

We got the info we needed into the spreadsheet, but we still needed to find a way to compare the different pension options.

Yes, we could see that waiting from one year to the next caused the lifetime payments to grow by over 7 percent, but was that growth worth it to give up one year or more of pension payments?

And how does taking the big amount of money through the lump-sum pension option compare to taking the monthly lifetime payments?

How do you compare $4,334 per month starting now versus $5,000 per month starting in two years?

How do you compare $547,439 now to $4,334 per month for the rest of your life?

It seems like you are comparing apples and oranges, but it's more like comparing one currency against another.

If you want to compare the value of the US dollar versus the Mexican peso or the euro, you need to learn the exchange rate. A lump-sum pension offer and a guaranteed lifetime monthly payment are really two different types of money, and you need to be able to compare them.

The easiest way I've found to do that is to turn to the financial markets and find out what that one-time, up-front, lump-sum amount would buy you in a monthly lifetime annuity payment from a private insurance company.

Just like you could choose to forego your promised monthly lifetime pension and instead get a lump sum of money up front, you could go to an insurance company and give them a lump sum of money up front so that they would then give you a guaranteed monthly lifetime payment.

In order to figure out the lump-sum versus monthly payout "exchange rate," go to a guaranteed income calculator online (I like using Schwab's).[3] Tell it how much your pension is willing to pay you on a certain date, and the calculator will tell you how much money it would take to have an insurance company pay you that dollar amount. I show you how to do this, in detail, in a video at JeremyKeil.com. Let's see how it works for Jeff and Michelle.

Jeff and I had all the info plugged into the spreadsheet, and then we went to the guaranteed income calculator to find out the true value of the monthly lifetime pension payments.

Here's how it looked when we compared the lump-sum option offered by the pension against the true present value of the lifetime pension options — both the value of the single life annuity (PV SLA) and the 100% joint survivor option (PV JT100).

Age	Lump Sum	PV SLA	PV JT 100	PV JT 100/ Lump	PV JT100- Lump
60	$547,439	$744,016	$704,876	129%	$157,437
61	$581,746	$792,338	$761,267		
62	$616,053	$768,436	$743,130		

We found that taking the monthly lifetime payments now was worth quite a bit more than taking the lump-sum option. The present value of the joint lifetime monthly payments was worth almost $160,000 more than the lump-sum option the pension would pay him.

Then we saw that taking the monthly pension one year after retiring versus taking it right away was worth roughly $55,000 more in "present value" than taking the monthly pension payments right away.

You might notice, as we did, that the single life annuity option, which pays more money when Jeff is alive and pays Michelle $0 every month when Jeff dies, was worth roughly 4% more in value than the 100% joint lifetime option. It's always good to find the numbers for each option, but as you can imagine, they were willing to "give up" that small difference to make sure Michelle was well protected.

We could see on our first spreadsheet that waiting two years would boost the pension by over 7 percent each year, and we knew what the pension was projecting for the lump-sum option over the next two years. But until we did the second spreadsheet and compared the value of the pension based on different options and different start dates, we couldn't really see which option and which timing were best for Jeff and Michelle.

Looking at how the pension changed over time is more work than most people do with their pension decision — most people just follow other people's hearsay instead of following the math of retirement.

When Jeff did the math, he found an extra $214,000 in present value by choosing to start his pension one year later and choosing to take the pension as a lifetime monthly payout instead of a one-time lump-sum payment. He helped his retirement to the tune of $214,000 just by getting a little more info than everyone else does, making some simple calculations, and filling out a form a certain way at a certain time.

Even though Jeff chose to wait one year to start his pension payments, that extra $214,000 in value from retirement decision-making gave him the confidence he needed to retire right away.

Now, not everyone will see a $200k-plus difference between one option and another. Every pension is different, every situation is different, and each year — or even each month — interest rates change, which makes the math on your pension decision change.

I created a pension decision worksheet, along with a video explaining how to use it. You can find both at JeremyKeil.com.

Jeff had wanted to retire the next April so that he and his wife, Michelle, could start traveling across America in their RV.

He was dreaming of traveling the country and *being* outside instead of going to work and *looking* outside. But until he started going through the math on his pension (and the other parts of retirement that you'll learn later on), he wasn't feeling confident in his ability to retire when he wanted to.

He wasn't willing to retire with so much uncertainty. He couldn't imagine leaving his job and his paycheck that showed up every two weeks without feeling confident that he had done enough to make the right decisions with his retirement.

Jeff was searching for answers on his pension, and he found them. In a way, Jeff was fortunate — he knew what info he needed to be looking for.

Others aren't as fortunate — they are facing retirement, relying on hearsay and traditions, and possibly missing out on hundreds of thousands of dollars from poor pension, Social Security, or tax decisions.

Maybe they retire, and they never learn what they were missing out on.

But more and more people I talk to tell me they are looking for a financial advisor, not to help them buy and sell stocks, but to help them find the blind spots in their planning.

They've tried just enough retirement planning on their own to realize they can't possibly learn all the angles in the amount of time they have left before their retirement date.

They think they've done a good job planning and projecting, but they are afraid they might have missed something in their spreadsheets.

They tell me, "I don't know what I don't know." And they aim to fill in the gaps.

CHAPTER 4

I Don't Know What I Don't Know

THERE'S SOMETHING HOLDING you back from retiring today. Maybe it's the fear of giving up your paycheck. Maybe it's the realization that you'll no longer be putting money *into* your accounts but taking money *out of* your accounts. Maybe you're worried about healthcare costs, Social Security running dry, and your taxes going up.

But above all, the biggest thing holding you back from retiring today is the fear of missing something.

The fear that, after all your saving, after all your planning and projecting and testing your spreadsheet, you'll retire and quickly realize you forgot to plan for something so obvious, so devastating to your financial future, that your retirement will never be as great as you thought it could be.

And I can't blame you for feeling this way. You've never retired before, you've never been taught to do it, and if you have a financial advisor currently, they probably haven't been much help in getting you ready to retire.

You've saved up $1 million, $2 million, $10 million-plus and you just don't know if it's enough, if you've done enough to make your retirement work.

You're not alone.

I hear it almost every single time I meet a new client.

"I've asked my investment guy what I should do with my Social Security or how to get health insurance, and he just can't give me a good answer."

"I asked my financial advisor if I should do a Roth conversion, and he told me he can't give me tax advice."

"I can't seem to get any answers. How am I supposed to know if I've done enough to retire?"

What's a good retirement saver to do?

Thankfully, there is hope, but it takes following a process, it takes a little time, and it takes some math!

I met Tim and Jennifer just this past summer. They were telling their friend they wanted to get ready for retirement, but they didn't know how to do it and didn't know where to turn. Thankfully, their friend had just attended one of my retirement planning webinars.

He told them I have a retirement planning process I walk people through, so they looked me up, booked an appointment, and drove out to my office.

Jennifer, a teacher, started the meeting by saying, "Tim would like us to retire, but I'm just not sure if we can. I'm six years younger than Tim, so I'll be in retirement a lot longer than he will be. What if I make it to 90 and run out of money, and I learn too late that we should have just worked another couple of years?

"I'd like to feel comfortable with us retiring, but I can't get any answers. I'm 53 years old, and the benefits specialist won't sit down with me unless I'm within one year of retirement. I've been there for over twenty years, and they won't give me the time of day! I want my ducks in a row. I'm not comfortable with retiring if I can't get any answers ahead of time!"

I asked Tim what he had done so far with his retirement planning.

"I'm a consultant, so for most years I have had a high income. We've just been stuffing as much money into my 401(k) as we can. I've got more in my 401(k) than I've ever had before, but I just don't know if it's enough.

"Since I turned 55, my 401(k) provider will meet with me once a year. Every year I sit down with them, they plug my numbers into their software, and they tell me I'm OK, but when I ask them what I should do to get ready for taxes in retirement or how I'm going to get health insurance before I'm 65, they don't have an answer for that."

I could tell the frustration had been building for quite some time.

I asked, "What would you like out of a financial advisor?"

Tim said, "It's great to *hear* that I'm OK, but how do I *know* that I'm going to be OK in retirement? I *want* to retire, but I need to *know* that I can retire. I'm a business consultant. I'm not a retirement consultant. I don't know these things.

"I don't even know what I don't know about retirement. I need an advisor who can show me what I need to do so I don't make any mistakes, and we don't run out of money when we're old."

I told them, "You're right on. There's a whole lot more to retirement than reaching a certain dollar amount in your 401(k). You're asking a lot of questions, but you're also wondering if you're asking the right questions.

"You've never retired before. I've never retired before, but I've helped hundreds of other people retire, and I've found that if you follow a process, you'll feel confident you checked all the boxes and made the right decisions when you do retire."

Tim and Jennifer looked at each other. I could just see the weight drop off their shoulders. Tim turned to me and said, "This must be the retirement process my friend was telling me about."

I said, "That's exactly it. Here's how we do it.

"First, we'll figure out how much you can **spend** in retirement, based on different retirement dates. We'll take a look at how much money could go into your checking account each month to spend, how much it might cost to get health insurance, and what your tax rate might be.

"Then, we'll look at how much you'll **make** in retirement and how you can try to maximize the amount you get over your whole lifetime. You each have a pension, and you each have Social Security. We'll project out how long you're likely to live in retirement and how taking your pension and Social Security at different ages would affect you when you first retire, and especially when you're down to just the surviving spouse.

"Next, we'll figure out how you can **keep** more of your money by lowering your lifetime taxes. You have different accounts with different tax rules — even your pension and Social Security have different tax rules. If we learn those rules and make use of your ability to choose which accounts to take money from and when to pay those taxes, I believe you can lower the taxes you can expect to pay over your lifetime.

"Then, we'll make sure how you **invest** your money is set up to cover both your short-term and your long-term needs. You've saved well in your 401(k), but you've been focused on taking money out in the future, not today. One of the biggest mistakes people make is thinking they need to either keep their 401(k) money totally invested for the future or totally invested for the right now.

"When you retire, you will need some money invested toward income right away, but you also still need to focus on your future growth. One of the best ways to make sure you can stay invested for future growth when the market eventually drops is to have enough money set aside for the short term to make sure you still get the income you want without having to sell your growth investments at a loss.

"Finally, we'll prepare for the legacy you will **leave** behind. You'd prefer to leave behind some money and not leave behind a mess. Planning for the big risks that might hurt your retirement will help you if things don't go as planned. And hopefully, things do go as planned, in which case you'll want to make sure your accounts and documents are ready so your kids can inherit the remainder of your money without creating family drama."

I asked, "What questions do you have?"

Jennifer said, "None. This is exactly what I need to feel comfortable with actually retiring."

Tim said, "Where do we start?"

I said, "You'll need to get some info, but it shouldn't be too hard. We'll just need to review:

- Both of your Social Security statements
- Your latest tax return
- Your 401(k) statement and something called your "Summary Plan Description" (SPD) that describes all the rules for your 401(k).
- Your pension info and the SPD for those pensions, too.
- Information on any retiree health plans you might have through work."

Tim said, "I think I can do that," and we set up a time to meet in two weeks.

I met with Tim and Jennifer four times throughout the summer and fall as we went through the different steps in order.

We refined the retirement income projections, and we dug deeper into the pension, Social Security, and investment options. We projected out their tax situation and planned for how their taxes are likely to look in retirement.

Each time we met, their confidence grew, as they moved further away from a fear of retirement and a fear that they didn't know enough or plan enough for retirement, and closer toward the joy that they were about to retire.

I talked to Tim on his 59½ birthday to take care of step 4 in the process — setting up the investments between short-term and long-term goals to match the planning from the first three steps.

Turning 59½ meant he could move his 401(k), as a rollover, to a traditional IRA and set his short-term money in interest rate accounts that were paying a higher rate than his 401(k) interest rate accounts. We could also set up his long-term growth money into diversified investments without being limited to the smaller number of growth funds available within the 401(k).

It's amazing how many people have no idea the significance of 59½ until they start the retirement planning process. It's the day that your traditional IRAs no longer have a 10 percent tax penalty when you take money out.

And for most people, it's the day when your company's 401(k) allows you to take money out of your 401(k) and roll it over to an IRA, even though you're still working there.

Tim knew the significance of the 59½ birthday, which is why he sent me a calendar invite six weeks earlier so that we could talk on that specific date. He wanted to get started on setting up his investments to match his planning as soon as he could.

I asked Tim if he was still planning on retiring on June 1. Even though he could go earlier, it made sense to keep working while his wife finished up the school year.

He smiled and said, "Absolutely! I've been talking to some other guys my age who wanted to retire this year, and the company asked them to delay and commit to retiring the next year. Those guys said they would wait, but I'm not going to do that. I've got it planned out. I know I can retire June 1, and there's no reason for me to delay. I've got my meeting with my boss next week, and there will be no talking me out of it — I'm ready to retire!"

Tim has mastered the retirement planning process, and he's going to retire when he wants to. Just six months ago, he and Jennifer didn't know how to go about planning for their retirement, but they asked around, they learned the process, and they followed the five steps.

I can just see Tim walking into that meeting next week. If it were a movie, you'd probably see him with a bit of a skip in his step as he walks into the office that day. When you get that kind of confidence because you've done the work, I say that you've become a Retirement Master.

You have mastered the habits of saving and investing as you worked throughout your career. You're faced with a retirement decision you've never faced before. You didn't know the way to retire with confidence. You didn't know what you didn't know, and you were afraid of making a mistake in your retirement planning.

But now you've learned the process, you've made the right moves, and you're ready to face retirement.

Tim and Jennifer became retirement masters by following the five steps it takes to get ready for retirement.

You'll learn those five steps and how to take them in the next chapter so that someday soon, you can call yourself a retirement master, too.

CHAPTER 5

How to Create Your Retirement Master Plan

I REMEMBER IT like it was yesterday: Monday, March 9, 2009. I was getting calls all day from worried clients. The stock market had been dropping for the past year and a half. That day, the market wasn't down that much, only 1 percent at its worst, but it was just another down day in a seemingly endless series of down days. The S&P 500 had dropped 12 percent over the past two weeks. The US stock market was now down a total of 57 percent since the October 10, 2007, high point.

It was a busy day, taking phone calls from some clients and reaching out proactively to others. I was telling people to "stay the course, invest for the long run. The worst time to sell is when the market is down." I must have talked to fifty people that day, but one in particular stood out.

I could hear the fear in Gary's voice when I picked up the phone. I knew it was him from the first word — we had talked virtually every day for the past two weeks.

"Jeremy, I've had it. I can't take it anymore. I want to get out of the stock market."

"It's not fun to watch your investments go down, Gary, but you're not retiring for another year." I told him, "Selling after the market drops in half is usually not a good way to go. I don't know when, but this market has got to recover."

"I know this is probably the wrong time to sell," said Gary, "but I can't watch my investments drop any further. I need to have something left for my retirement — if I'll even be able to retire. I wish I had sold two weeks ago when I called you then. Now I'm down 8 percent more in just two weeks! I want out. Please don't try to talk me out of it. You need to sell my investments right now."

Gary's fear was turning to anger. While he was a bit angry that I had convinced him not to sell in October 2008 and again in February 2009, he was probably angrier with himself. We had met in spring 2008 and his plan was to retire in two years. I had laid out my suggestion that, because he was within three to five years of retiring, he should consider selling some long-term growth investments and move the right amount to some short-term interest investments that were out of the stock market.

Gary liked the idea, but with his investments down about 10 percent from the fall 2007 peak, he said, "Let's wait until the market recovers, and then we'll take some profits and move it to cash."

Now here we were, just about one year later, and instead of having cashed in a small portion of his investments just 10 percent lower than the all-time market high, Gary wanted to sell everything he had and move it to cash after his investments had lost almost half of their value.

I tried one more idea, "What if we sell just half to cash, Gary? That way, if the market goes down, you'll be happy you put half in cash, but if the market goes up, you'll be happy you kept half in stocks."

He wasn't having any of it. "Sell everything to cash. I don't want to hear any more. Investing for the long run hasn't helped me over the last year. I need to know I have something left in my name."

I told Gary I would sell his investments. I turned to my computer, placed the trades, and told Gary, "All the sells went through. You'll get a confirmation that your account is all in cash tomorrow."

Gary said, "Thank you," and hung up the phone. I turned to my business partner at the time and said, "Gary couldn't take it anymore. He sold to cash. I bet today is the bottom." And unfortunately for Gary, I was correct.

Three weeks later, at the end of March, the S&P 500 was up 18 percent. At the end of the year, the US stock market was up 65 percent from its bottom of March 9, 2009 — the exact day Gary sold out.

And while Gary's story is tragic, and his phone call was stressful to me and, even more importantly, to him, what stands out to me about the Great Financial Crisis are the phone calls I didn't get.

As I did my normal client meetings throughout 2009, I remember talking to people like Mike and Lisa, who I mentioned in chapter 1. They had a plan in place that focused on the proper amount of money for them in short-term and long-term investments. They never called me in a panic during that financial crisis, like so many others.

I remember, too, Jim and Linda. I met them in 2006, and they told me they'd like to retire in 2013, seven years down the road, at age 62.

Jim asked me, "What should we do to get ready for retirement?"

I told him how I approached retirement, similar to what I told Mike and Lisa. I showed them how it made sense for Jim to delay Social Security for a few years, even though he planned on retiring at age 62.

Linda asked, "Where do we get income from if Jim delays his Social Security?"

I showed them that it often made sense to do a "Social Security Bridge," which means you take money out of the stock market and set it aside in short-term investments so that you can live off your short-term investments for a few years, then turn on Social Security after that.

Meanwhile, your long-term investments are still invested toward the long term because you have the short-term investments paying out to your checking account in the beginning years of retirement.

Jim was seven years from retirement, which for many people is too early to start moving money from growth to income. But when I told Jim about the idea of a Social Security Bridge and setting aside some money today to guarantee he had enough set aside for the first three years of his retirement, his eyes lit up.

He said, "I know that I'm seven years away from retirement, but I don't want to mess around — I want to retire at 62 whether the market is up or down."

I met with Jim and Linda at their house that summer of 2009. The market was starting to turn around but was still far below its high point from just two years earlier. We talked through their investments, their plans for retirement in four years that still looked on track, and their plans for where to get health insurance when they retired. At the end of the meeting, I asked them a question I ask almost every time.

"What other questions might you have for me?"

"None," Jim replied, "But I really need to say thank you. Thank you for getting me to move money out of the stock market three years ago. That money I have set aside out of the market has turned out to be a great idea."

"Don't thank me," I said, "All I did was share a few ideas, and you really jumped on the idea of moving some long-term growth money over to short-term investments, so you knew you had those first few years of retirement covered."

Linda said, "Well, either way, I'm so glad Jim took that chunk of money out of the stock market. You don't know how many of our friends are checking their 401(k) every day, and they're stressing out like crazy. I know the market is down big, but honestly, we just don't worry about it. We've got a plan, and we're following it. Thank you."

I said, "You're welcome," packed up my computer and files, and then drove the thirty minutes back to the office with that conversation replaying in my mind.

Especially the part when she said, "We don't worry about it. We've got a plan, and we're following it."

By the time I got back to the office, I had made up my mind about two things:

1. I needed to keep finding, keep using, and keep refining ways to better help people use the retirement planning process I had been developing over the years.
2. I needed to get that process in front of as many people as possible.

Over the next few years, I presented the retirement planning process at hundreds of seminars I hosted at my office, at hotels, and in church basements.

I didn't use a projector or fancy slides, I just stood in front of a flip chart, drawing out and talking through the five steps to take to be able to retire with confidence. Each time, I discovered that a different word or example I used was helpful, or perhaps unhelpful, in explaining how to retire and what steps to take.

Eventually, I started sharing this process on my *Retire Today* podcast and then on the *Mr. Retirement* YouTube channel.

I call this process your Retirement Master Plan because once you learn and follow its five simple steps, you'll feel more confident in your retirement plans, you'll conquer your retirement journey, and you'll become a retirement master.

Here's a snapshot of the five steps, which we'll cover in the following chapters:

$ STEP 1: SPEND

Discover how much income you need and when you could retire.

📅 STEP 2: MAKE

Maximize what you make in retirement from Social Security, pensions, and other income sources.

⌄ STEP 3: KEEP

Lower your lifetime taxes by using the tax rules to your advantage.

📊 STEP 4: INVEST

Choose the right mix of short-term and long-term investments.

∞ STEP 5: LEAVE

Leave your spouse and kids the gift of a well-thought-out legacy instead of the burden of an inheritance mess.

RETIREMENT MASTER PLAN

1. $ SPEND How Much You Need & When.

2. 📅 MAKE Max Your Monthly Lifetime Income.

3. ⌄ KEEP Lower Your Lifetime Tax Bill.

4. 📊 INVEST Short & Long Term Money.

5. ∞ LEAVE Protect Against Risks & Create Family Legacy.

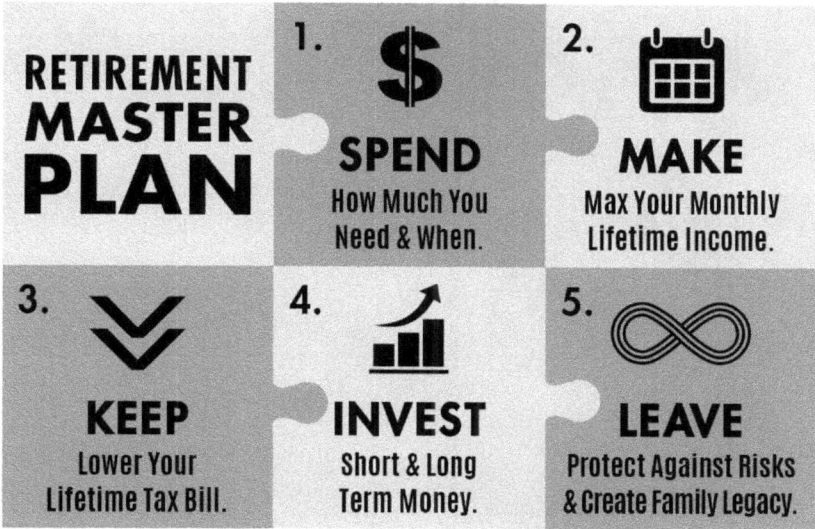

And now let's dive into the details of each step, starting with step 1: Spend. Notice how we start with your spending, not your investments. Let me tell you why.

CHAPTER 6

Retirement Master Plan
$ STEP 1: SPEND

WHEN YOU'RE CREATING any financial plan, you need to know what you are solving for. What are you trying to optimize?

If you're in a corporation, you're often solving for the net present value, which is somewhat simple. You just plug in some projections of future cash flows, add in an interest rate, and use Excel to solve.

If you're saving for retirement, you're probably trying to grow your money until your retirement date. This is also somewhat simple. Just plug in how much you're saving, assume an interest rate, and tell the spreadsheet when you plan to retire.

When you're solving for retirement income, you're trying to get the most income over your entire lifetime. Unlike our first two scenarios, this problem is incredibly hard to solve. You probably don't know how much money you need, and you definitely don't know exactly how long you'll need it for.

Let's tackle the "how much money you need" part of this problem first.

- Go online to your checking account.
- Look to see how much money you get every two weeks for your take-home paycheck.
- That's how much money you will need to show up in your checking account every two weeks when you're retired.

Now, it gets a little more complicated than that, but look at your checking account and see what you get paid every two weeks.

- Chances are, what goes into your checking account gets spent.
- Chances are, you'd love to keep spending that same amount of money on the things you're buying now once you've retired.
- That's your goal, then: replace your paycheck amount in your checking account, without working.

Looking at your take-home paycheck is way easier than tracking your spending, and I've found it's way more effective than building your budget from the ground up.

WHY YOU DON'T NEED TO BUDGET

I've seen hundreds of retirement budgets people have created as they get ready to retire, and they are consistently off by thousands of dollars every month.

Most people start from the ground up, writing out their expenses like property taxes, groceries, and the internet.

Then they start estimating what those costs will be, and they are wildly off.

It's not a bad idea to think about your spending. It's not a bad idea to track your spending. But what happens almost every time is that either:

- You think you have to create a budget in order to retire, and you hate creating a budget, so you end up avoiding the retirement planning process altogether, or
- You create budget line items that look good on paper. You say, "If I can get this dollar amount every month, I'll be fine," and then you put down cost estimates that assume you never go out to eat, your car never breaks down, and you never do anything fun in retirement.

Now, there are some budgets that are more believable, but they are few and far between, and they are still off by thousands of dollars every month.

A few years ago, Thomas came into my office and asked if I wanted to see his retirement budget.

I told him, "I've found it's more helpful to learn your two-week take-home pay amount and how much you put into investments from your bank account. That info will help us calculate how much you need in retirement."

Thomas said, "My take-home pay is $4,000 every two weeks into my checking account, and on average, I save about $20,000 per year into my brokerage investment account."

Thomas then said, "I have been using Quicken for the past two years so that I could plan for my retirement budget. On average, my spending comes to almost exactly $7,000 per month."

I told Thomas, "That is so great you took the time to track and plan out your spending. That is a budget I'm willing to believe, except that every budget I see through a tracker like Quicken is missing two key pieces of information.

"Every tracker like Quicken only looks at how much money goes into your checking account. Two of your biggest expenses in retirement will be your health insurance costs and your income taxes. Both of those come out of your paycheck before it hits your checking account. Your Quicken is absolutely correct that you spend $7,000 per month on average out of your checking account. We need to take that number, and then we also need to plan for your health insurance costs and your tax costs on top of that."

"You're right," said Thomas, "I've been planning on $7,000 per month in my spreadsheets, but I wasn't planning for my health insurance and tax costs. I'm way underestimating!"

"That's OK," I told him, "It looks like you've been such a good saver that I'm sure you'll have enough, but we do want to be accurate and make sure we have line items in your plan for your everyday spending that you've been tracking AND those health and tax costs."

"Thanks!" said Thomas. "I'm glad you showed me that. By the way, why did you want to know my take-home pay and how much I put into my investment account?"

"Because that shows me your monthly spending without having to create a budget or track it for two years," I told him. "Your take-home pay is $4,000 every two weeks. $4,000 × 26 is $104,000. You save about $20,000 into your investment account every year. $104,000 - $20,000 is $84,000, so your monthly spending is $7,000 per month, the same as your Quicken number."

INCOME − SAVINGS = SPENDING

INCOME	
Take Home	$4,000
Every 2 Weeks	x 26
Annual	$104,000
− Savings	− $20,000
Annual Spending	$84,000
Convert to Monthly	÷ 12
= MONTHLY SPENDING	$7,000

Thomas introduced me to the most detailed, down to the penny, spending spreadsheet I've ever seen in over two decades as a financial advisor. And with all his diligent effort his budget tracking was no different than this formula:

Income − Savings = Spending

SAVINGS: WHAT DOES THAT REALLY MEAN?

Before we dive into the specifics, we need to talk about what I mean by "savings." Virtually everyone I talk to says something along the lines of, "I save $2,000 per month into my savings account."

I then say, "That's so great! You must be living on $2,000 less per month than your take-home pay. You must also have $100,000 saved up from the past four years."

They then reply, "Are you kidding me? I'm barely break-ing even with my paycheck — I'm not living on less than that! And $100 grand in savings? I might have a few thousand in my checking, but I hardly have anything in savings!"

How can that be? How can someone who "saves $2,000 per month" into their savings account have so little saved up?

It's the same reason I don't believe any personal retire-ment budget I see — it's easy to remember the one-time ac-tions like, "I automatically put $2,000 per month into my savings account," and it's incredibly hard to remember the little actions that add up, like grabbing cash from the ATM, or paying property taxes, or paying insurance, or going away for the weekend, or giving your kids a few hundred bucks at Christmas, or putting the down payment on that big cruise you're taking next year.

Most everyone I talk to consistently sets aside money into their savings account each month, and then sporadically takes the money out of savings throughout the year.

But that's not "saving." It's "escrowing."

It's a wise choice to set aside money every month for the big one-time expenses that happen throughout the year, but those expenses are still part of your retirement spending plan.

Since it's easy to fool yourself into thinking that your monthly "escrow" into savings counts as "saving" (and not spending) when you're creating your retirement spending plan, another great way to see how much of your paycheck you truly spend, and how much you truly save, is to look at your savings account balance a year ago and then today.

If your savings account has more money today than one year ago, then you were saving out of your paycheck. If it has less money than last year, then you probably spent more than you earned in the past twelve months. What you'll most likely see though is that despite saving $2,000 per month into your savings account, your balance is relatively the same today as twelve months ago, which is why I always say:

What goes into your checking account gets spent.

What goes into your checking account gets spent.

If you haven't created your budget, if you've been putting off retirement planning because you didn't want to go through the drudgery of tracking your spending, I hereby, within my power as "Mr. Retirement," absolve you from ever having to create a budget.

You don't have to create a budget to create your retirement spending plan. But you still need to create a retirement spending plan. Here's how you do it.

You don't have to create a budget to create your retirement spending plan.

HOW TO CREATE YOUR RETIREMENT SPENDING PLAN

1. Discover Your Monthly Lifestyle Amount

Since what goes into your checking account most likely gets spent, and most income in retirement gets paid out monthly (like pensions, Social Security, and investment withdrawals), you'll need to convert your bi-weekly take-home pay to a monthly amount.

If you have $3,250 every two weeks showing up in your checking account, then multiply $3,250 × 26 = $84,500.

$84,500 ÷ 12 months = ~$7,000 per month.

This is your monthly lifestyle amount — the amount you spend on a monthly basis to support your ongoing lifestyle.

Put that into your retirement planning as a line item. Since you'll keep spending this money throughout your lifetime, and what you buy today will probably cost more next year, you'll need to account for this being a lifetime expense that grows with inflation.

Are you someone who "saves" a certain dollar amount every month? Do you put perhaps $750 every paycheck directly into your savings account, and then throughout the year, use that money for things like insurance, property taxes, and vacations? Then it would be great to create another line item for your annual expense items.

In this case, $750 per paycheck × 26 = $19,500, which I'll round up below.

Make sure to add an inflation assumption going forward for both of these line items. Quite often, you might assume 3 percent for inflation.

Your retirement spending plan might start with these two line items:

Monthly Lifestyle Amount:	$7,000 per month, with 3% inflation
Annual Expense Items:	$20,000 per year, with 3% inflation

2. Research Your Health Insurance Costs and Add a Line Item for This

Why put health insurance as a separate line item? Because your health insurance costs change over time.

Perhaps one of you in a couple is on Medicare, and the other one isn't. Perhaps you have a retiree healthcare account from your employer that will subsidize your costs for several years. And if there are two of you and one of you passes away, then that person's health insurance costs go away.

Put in a separate health insurance line item, perhaps several different line items. And make sure to add an inflation assumption going forward, probably at a higher rate than your standard inflation adjustment, perhaps 4 or 5 percent.

Your health insurance line items might look like this:

Pre-65 Health Insurance:	$1,000 per month per person, with 5% inflation, until age 65
Post-65 (Medicare) Health Insurance:	$400 per month per person, with 5% inflation, starting at age 65

3. Add a Line Item for Your Expected Income Tax Costs

Now this is a line item I'm concerned about. Most people ask me what tax rate to assume in retirement. I don't like using a specific tax rate in retirement planning.

One reason is that there is no single tax rate that is good for all people to assume. Another reason is that your taxes change over time, especially when your life changes — taxes are not constant!

And the most important reason is that when you assume a specific tax rate, let's say 20 percent, and you add that into your retirement spending plan, you take away the idea that you can plan out and reduce your lifetime tax bill.

I prefer to use a retirement planning software program that accounts for your personal tax situation, how it changes over time, AND suggests how you could rearrange your tax situation in order to lower your lifetime tax bill.

But if you're doing this on your own, then a decent estimate is to look at your tax return last year and use your effective tax rate for federal, state, and (if it applies) local income taxes.

For example, if you made $162,000 last year and you paid $17,000 in federal and $7,000 in state taxes, that $24,000 total income taxes ÷ $162,000 income = ~15 percent effective tax rate.

And don't forget that if your income is going to grow each year, your income taxes are likely to grow each year.

Your income tax estimate line item might look like this:

Income Tax Estimate:	
$162,000 total income needed, 15% effective tax rate:	$24,000 per year, with 3% inflation

4. Calculate Your Non-Lifetime Expenses

Many of your expenses, in fact, I would say the vast majority of your expenses, will follow this pattern:

- Your spending starts on day 1 of retirement.
- The cost of that spending grows every year with inflation.
- That spending lasts as long as you do.

But many of your expenses don't follow that pattern, and I often see incorrect assumptions in someone's retirement spending plan because of this.

Some assumptions make it seem like you need more income in retirement than you really do, and then you calculate that you can't afford to retire, when, in fact, you can. Often, these assumptions are related to your mortgage.

Other assumptions make it seem like you won't be spending on certain line items, when, in fact, you are very likely going to buy those things, and then you retire without a spending plan to help you afford those things. Often, these assumptions are related to home renovations or travel, since, in retirement, you'll either be traveling more (and spending more) *or* you'll be at home more, finally fixing and upgrading all the things you couldn't get to while you were working.

To complete your retirement spending plan, you'll need to calculate the expenses that will go away or start in retirement.

Expenses That Often Go Away In Retirement

If you have a mortgage and plan to pay it off before you retire, you don't have to plan for your mortgage in retirement.

Or maybe you have a mortgage that you'll keep in retirement. You don't need to have that in your lifestyle spending line item, because that line item is designed to last as long as you do and grow with inflation.

Your mortgage doesn't grow with inflation, and it will go away when it's paid off. Imagine you're currently getting $7,000 per month into your checking account and sending out $2,000 per month to your mortgage, which will be paid off in ten years.

That's not $7,000 per month + inflation for the rest of your life that you need to plan for. That's $5,000 per month + inflation for the rest of your life and it's $2,000 per month, no inflation, for however long is left on your mortgage, in this example, ten years.

You might have listed your monthly lifestyle amount as:

Monthly Lifestyle Amount:	$7,000 per month, with 3% inflation

Instead, you should get more detailed to account for the mortgage payment, which has no inflation cost and stops at a specific point in time.

Instead, your monthly lifestyle amount should be updated to:

Monthly Lifestyle Amount:	$5,000 per month, with 3% inflation until the end
Monthly Mortgage Cost:	$2,000 per month, with 0% inflation, ending in ten years

Expenses That Often Start In Retirement

I've seen two things happen to people who retire and discover they have fifty-two weeks of vacation each year instead of just five.

Either they use their newfound free time to travel to all the places they've always wanted to go to, or they sit around their house looking at all the things they've wanted to update but never had the time for.

Either way, it costs money — money you weren't spending previously.

And often, they do both!

Plan For Added Travel Expenses

Many people I talk to have a dream list of all the places they'd like to go on vacation once they retire. They might do one big vacation each year now, but when they go from five weeks' worth of vacation days while working to fifty-two weeks of vacation days when they are retired, they plan to travel a lot more.

Make sure to budget for these extra vacation costs, AND also realize that quite often, you'll only have the energy and desire to do these vacations for the first half of your retirement.

If you're planning on taking one extra $5,000 vacation per year for the rest of your life, you're probably much better off planning for two extra vacations ($10,000 annually) for the first half of retirement instead.

Talk to your older friends who are retired, or perhaps look at how your parents experienced retirement. You'll probably see two things:

1. They traveled a lot less in the second half of retirement than in the first half of retirement.
2. They traveled a whole lot less after the first spouse passed away.

Learn something from your elders: Plan your vacations, take your vacations, budget for your vacations for when you're younger, and if there are two of you, for when there are two of you.

The vacation line of your retirement spending plan might look like this:

Extra Travel:	$10,000 per year, with 3% inflation, for fifteen years, with the cost dropping in half when one spouse passes away

Plan For Added Home Renovation Costs

Maybe you don't have plans to renovate your kitchen or bathroom right now, but I've found that as soon as you retire, you either spend more time *outside* of the house traveling or *inside* your house, looking around at all the things you want to fix!

If you have plans to renovate your house when you retire, you need to create a separate home renovation line item within your retirement spending plan. It might look like:

Home Renovation Costs:	
Kitchen Remodel:	$50,000 in the first year
Bathroom Remodel:	$25,000 in the second year

Or you might want to buy a vacation home. You might be saving up and planning to pay cash, or maybe you'll be getting a second mortgage. Your line item might look like this:

Vacation Home:	$500,000 in year one

Or

Vacation Home:	$100,000 down payment in year one
	$3,100 per month, 0% inflation, for thirty years

When it comes to your Retirement Master Plan, the number one thing you're solving for is how much income you'll need.

You might not need to budget. In fact, I'd encourage you NOT to create a budget. I have yet to meet a retirement budget that's 100 percent correct. You'll probably be vastly underestimating how much you'll spend, and you'll almost definitely forget to include your health insurance and/or tax costs.

Instead, use the guidelines in this chapter to create your retirement spending plan based on how much you're spending already, as well as on your thoughtful consideration of your health insurance costs, your tax costs, your extra travel and house costs, and how they will all change over time.

Your retirement spending plan should include all the components of your expected spending, broken down based on how long you expect the spending to last and what inflation rate you want to project. Here is what it might look like:

RETIREMENT SPENDING PLAN (EXAMPLE)

SPENDING	Monthly Lifestyle Amount:	$5,000/Month, 3% Inflation → End
	Monthly Mortgage Cost:	$2,000/Month, 0% Inflation → 10 Years
	Annual Expense Items:	$20,000/Year, 3% Inflation → End

| HEALTH COSTS | Pre-65 Health Insurance: | $1,000/Month Per Person, 5% Inflation → 65 |
| | Post-65 (Medicare) Health Insurance: | $400/Month Per Person, 5% Inflation. 65 → End |

| TAXES | $162,000 Income 15% Effective Tax Rate: | $24,000/Year, 3% Inflation → End |

NON-LIFETIME	Extra Travel:	$10,000/Year, 3% Inflation → 15 Years
	Kitchen Remodel:	$50,000 → Year 1
	Bathroom Remodel:	$25,000 → Year 2

Now that you've created your retirement spending plan, it's time to start funding your plan. The first place to start is with guaranteed income sources like Social Security and your pension, if you have one.

You've worked hard for your Social Security, and your pension. You deserve to get the most you can.

The more you can maximize your Social Security and pension with decisions like when and how you file, the less you have to worry about whether your investments are able to create the income you need to meet your retirement spending plan.

CHAPTER 7

Retirement Master Plan
📅 STEP 2: MAKE

JUST BECAUSE YOU stop going to work when you retire, it doesn't mean you stop making money.

You'll almost definitely be making money from Social Security. Perhaps there will be two Social Security payments if there are two of you as a couple. You might even be getting a pension.

Getting the most out of your lifetime income sources, like Social Security and pensions, is going to be crucial for your retirement success.

Which is why the next step, after first creating your retirement spending plan, is to create your lifetime income plan.

When you file for Social Security and when you file for your pension are often one-time

> Just because you stop going to work when you retire, it doesn't mean you stop making money.

decisions, one-time actions. You fill out a piece of paper, you check a box, and you can never change those decisions for the rest of your life.

You need to make sure you get your Social Security and pension decisions correct. How and when you fill out your Social Security and pension paperwork could make you $100,000 or more in extra lifetime income compared to the average American.

More likely, though, the decisions retirees make about their Social Security and pensions *cost* them $100,000 or more in lost benefits compared to how they perhaps should have chosen to file.

A recent study by economist Larry Kotlikoff[4] suggests that your Social Security decisions, especially if you're in a couple, could cost you $182,370 in lifetime benefits!

He found that only 4 percent of people filed for Social Security in a way that was "optimal" for them, based on their life expectancy and financial situation.

Since pensions are becoming less prevalent, and there is no universal formula for pensions, it's hard for researchers to determine how well people are doing with their pension-claiming strategies — but I bet the results are similar. I wouldn't be surprised if only 4 percent of people claiming their pension are doing it in a way that follows the math on how to get the most out of their pension over their lifetime.

From what I've learned from talking to hundreds of retirees, the reason they make the "suboptimal" choice with Social Security and their pensions is that they more often rely on hearsay and myths than on the math.

If you'd like to get more out of your hard-earned Social Security and pension, follow the steps below.

HOW TO MAXIMIZE YOUR SOCIAL SECURITY

Here are a few things to keep in mind regarding your Social Security, especially if there are two of you as part of a married couple.

If you are a married couple where one spouse has a higher amount of Social Security than the other, when both of you have filed, you're getting both dollar amounts. But when there's only one of you around because the first person has passed away, the lower of the two benefits goes away.

The higher benefit lasts longer at a higher amount, and the lower benefit doesn't last as long at a lower amount.

The older individual benefit is important because your benefit grows as you get older, and if you're already older, you get to those ages first!

And while both the higher and lower benefits grow at 8 percent every year, 8 percent on a higher number is a higher number!

Therefore, for a couple, the higher Social Security benefit is the more important benefit.

If you want to maximize your lifetime income from Social Security, you'll want to maximize your higher benefit, especially if that benefit is from the older individual.

HOW TO MAXIMIZE SOCIAL SECURITY WHEN YOU'RE SINGLE

I talk more about the Social Security decisions of a couple, as I often see the most mistakes being made there. If you're single, though, keep in mind two things:

1. Just because you are single now doesn't mean you were always single. If you are divorced or widowed, then you might have access to ex-spouse or survivor benefits, and how you coordinate the two (or more) benefits available to you often follows the exact same logic as the way to maximize a couple's benefits.

2. If you're single, you'll be relying solely on your own Social Security and retirement decisions. Often, singles take their Social Security ASAP because "there's no one else to get my money." But consider flipping that thought around: there's no one else you can rely on, therefore your decisions are even more important!

    Don't fall into the traps of hearsay and myths. You deserve to get the most out of your hard-earned Social Security. Follow the same guidelines around life expectancy and the role of Social Security within your retirement planning as the couple-focused examples I use.

In order to maximize the amount of Social Security over your lifetime, it's important to watch out for the top three Social Security myths:

Social Security Myth #1: It Doesn't Matter When You File, It All Evens Out

This myth is based on a kernel of truth. Yes, the decrease or increase in your Social Security for filing earlier or later is supposed to average out; however, those percentages are based on life expectancy and interest rates when Social Security last had a big change: 1983!

From 1983 to 2025, life expectancy has increased by four years. Social Security was trying to keep things even, but then people started living longer, so the increased amount for waiting to file lasts longer.

From 1983 to 2025, interest rates dropped from the teens to the single digits! Social Security was trying to keep things even, but then interest rates dropped, and the amount of interest you could get from putting your Social Security in the bank today no longer matched up with the increase in payment from waiting on Social Security.

Right now, waiting to file from age 62 to age 70 increases your benefit by roughly 7.4 percent every year.

In 2025, based on current life expectancy and interest rates, that benefit increase should be cut in half if we're trying to even out the lifetime benefits, no matter when you file.

Waiting on Social Security or taking it early doesn't even out right now — the promised increase for every year of waiting to file for Social Security is basically double what it should be.

Social Security Myth #2: You Can File Early, Invest Your Benefits, And Get A Better Return

I hear this myth a lot, especially when someone has created a spreadsheet to map out their "break-even age." There are three big factors that make the "file early and invest" math a lot more complicated than one might assume.

1. When you invest in the stock market, it is risky, and you don't know if you'll get the rate of return you assume. Meanwhile, Social Security is guaranteed by the US government.
2. When you delay Social Security, the amount you are waiting to take grows with inflation. Meanwhile, stock market investing is not guaranteed to grow with inflation.
3. Delaying the higher benefit in a couple creates a time frame that doesn't matter whether *you* make it to the

"break-even age." It needs to incorporate the spousal survivor benefit and the chance that *either one of you* makes it to the "break-even age."

I have yet to see someone's break-even or a "take early and invest" spreadsheet that accounts for all three of these factors. In fact, almost every spreadsheet I've seen doesn't even have one of these factors accounted for.

I've come across only one analysis that considers all three factors, conducted by Dr. David Blanchett.[5] He found that for a couple with an average life expectancy, their investments would need to earn an 8 percent annual return just to break even with the benefits of delaying Social Security.

While an 8 percent return is possible in the stock market, it's not guaranteed. On the other hand, delaying Social Security provides a guaranteed lifetime income, with benefits adjusted for inflation. That's why many retirement researchers believe that, in most cases, delaying Social Security is the better choice.

Social Security Myth #3: When You Delay Filing, the Odds Are Low That You'll Reach the Break-Even Point

So many people say these exact words to me: "The break-even age for waiting on Social Security is 80. What are the odds I'll make it there?" And then they shrug their shoulders as if it's impossible to know the odds.

My response is, "Let's find out those odds!"

The first thing you should do when looking at your Social Security decision is try to determine your life expectancy.

A tool like the Actuaries Longevity Illustrator[6] can be a huge help. Not only will it give you an idea of how long you might live, which is a key factor in your retirement planning, but it also can give you the "odds" of making it to certain ages.

Let's take a look at the odds of making it to age 80.

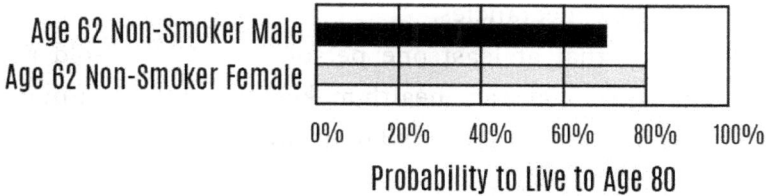

Age 62 Non-Smoker Male
Age 62 Non-Smoker Female

0%   20%   40%   60%   80%   100%

Probability to Live to Age 80

For a 62-year-old non-smoking male of average health, the odds of making it to age 80 are roughly 70 percent. For a 62-year-old non-smoking female of average health, the odds of making it to age 80 are roughly 80 percent.

Both of those are pretty good odds. One way to think about this is that if you delay filing for Social Security, you are taking the 75 percent probability bet (I'm averaging the male and female odds). And if you choose to take Social Security early, you are taking the 25 percent probability bet.

If you could walk into a casino with odds of winning at 75 percent, you'd never walk out! Yet many people are walking into Social Security offices across the country, asking to file for Social Security earlier than perhaps they should and basing their decision on odds that are unlikely to work out.

Here's what's even crazier — if there are two of you in a couple, and you are talking about the higher benefit, that benefit won't last as long as *you* last; that benefit will last as long as *either of you* lasts.

While, on average, *you* will live to the average age.

When there are two of you, on average, *one* of you will live shorter, and *one* of you will live longer than the individual average.

That's why, when you're looking at your Social Security decision for the higher benefit, you need to look at the odds that either of you will still be living at that break-even age — that's called your "joint life expectancy."

Because, on average, one of you will live longer than aver-age, your joint life expectancy will be longer than each of your individual life expectancies.

The odds that at least one person in a 62-year-old non-smoking couple of average health makes it to that often-quoted break-even age of 80 are over 90 percent!

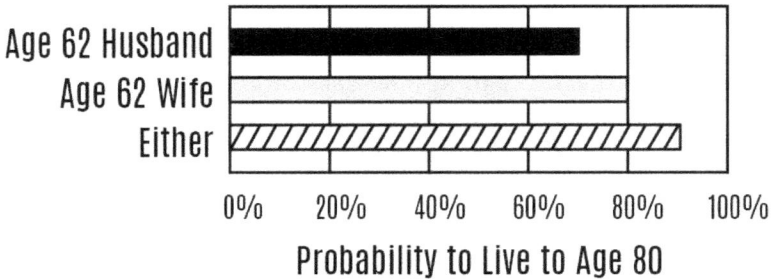

Probability to Live to Age 80

When you shrug your shoulders and say, "What are the odds that it's worth it to delay that higher benefit?" the answer could easily be over 90 percent!

Now, you should look at your own personal health and couple situation and get your own odds, but generally speak-ing, when you delay Social Security, the odds are usually in your favor.

Social Security is not an investment. You can't create a spreadsheet or guarantee that taking Social Security later or, perhaps, taking it early and investing is the better choice. But you do want to push the odds in your favor.

Which leads us to the one thing you need to remember when you're making your Social Security decision:

Treat your Social Security decision based on the true offi-cial name of the Social Security retirement program: Old-Age and Survivors Insurance.

To do that, keep these three things in mind:

1. Social Security is there to help you in your old age.
2. Social Security is there to help the surviving spouse.
3. Social Security is insurance in case you live longer than you expect, in case inflation goes up more than you expect, or in case your investments don't do as well as you expect.

> **Treat your Social Security decision based on the true official name of the Social Security retirement program: Old-Age and Survivors Insurance.**

Keep those three things in mind when you make your Social Security decision, and you'll be well on your way toward collecting that $180,000 in lost benefits the average couple misses out on over their lifetime because they filed at the wrong time.

HOW TO MAXIMIZE YOUR PENSION

Maximizing your pension involves a lot of the same concepts as maximizing your Social Security, but with one big wrinkle: you can probably choose to take your pension as a lump-sum, up-front, one-time payout, and you can't choose that with Social Security.

The three main principles that help you make Social Security decisions also apply to making your pension decision. Your pension is there to:

1. Help you in your old age
2. Help your surviving spouse
3. Act as insurance in case you live longer than you expect or your investments don't go as well as you expect

Your pension *may* help you match inflation, although most of the time it is a level monthly payment that does not increase with inflation.

Since the main difference between Social Security and pensions is the likely option to take a lump-sum payout, let's focus our time there.

When you're making that decision, it's very easy to look at that big dollar amount of the lump-sum option and think of how great it would be to have $200,000, $500,000, or more in your hand, especially when you compare that to your monthly lifetime payment, which is maybe $1,000, $2,000, or $5,000 per month for the rest of your life.

Whatever the dollar amount is, I guarantee that lump-sum payout will be a bigger dollar amount than that lifetime payment each month.

How do you possibly make that comparison? You really need to look at it as if it's almost like a currency.

If you go to Europe or Mexico and you're comparing dollars and euros or dollars and pesos, you can't figure out which is worth more unless you know what the exchange rate is.

What does it look like to actually exchange and transfer your dollars over to a different currency? You've got to do the same comparison between your lump-sum option and your monthly lifetime payment.

When you work with a financial advisor, they should be able to show you exactly how to compare the big one-time payment and the pension's monthly amount. I say "should be able to" because the answer is simple math; however, most of the time, they aren't able to help you here — either because they don't know how or, unfortunately, because they have a huge incentive for you to take the lump-sum pension option.

Your financial advisor likely makes money when you take a lump-sum payout, but they probably make no money when you take the monthly pension option.

Keep this in the front of your mind when your advisor tells you to take the lump-sum pension option. They might start charging you 1 percent or more to manage that money, or maybe they'll even sell you an annuity and make a 5–8 percent commission!

> **Your financial advisor likely makes money when you take a lump-sum payout, but they probably make no money when you take the monthly pension option.**

Now, there may be very good reasons to take the lump-sum option, but remember that the financial advisor's financial incentives could play a big part in their recommendation.

How do you make that comparison? How do you figure out the "exchange rate" between the lump-sum dollar amount and the monthly lifetime amount?

Thankfully, there are plenty of insurance companies on the open market who act like pension companies, and they will tell you the exact "exchange rate," if you ask.

You can go to places like the Charles Schwab Income Annuity Estimator,[7] the Fidelity Guaranteed Income Estimator,[8] or ImmediateAnnuities.com[9] to get real-time pricing so that you can make that comparison.

I created a pension decision worksheet, along with a video explaining how to use it to make your pension comparison. You can download the worksheet and watch the video at JeremyKeil.com.

But here's a quick snapshot of how making this pension comparison helps you make the best pension decision for you. You might be a 65-year-old male living in Wisconsin, and your pension gives you two main choices (we'll talk about survivorship options later on):

- Take a monthly pension of $2,000 per month for the rest of your life, with no survivorship, or
- Take a $280,000 lump sum right now.

How can you possibly make the comparison between $280,000 once versus $2,000 per month for the rest of your life?

I went to Schwab's calculator (on March 13, 2025) and saw that it would take a $318,470 investment with an annuity company to generate $2,000 per month for the rest of this person's life.

Here's how it looks now that you have all the info:

PENSION DECISION SPREADSHEET

Age	Monthly Payment	Lump Sum Option	Present Value of Monthly Payment
65	$2,000	$280,000	$318,470
			Market value is $38,470 higher.

Notice how the market value of the guaranteed lifetime monthly payments is worth roughly 14 percent higher than the lump-sum option from the pension company.

Now, just because the value of the lifetime monthly payments is worth more than the lump sum available right now doesn't mean that this person should automatically take the monthly pension, but comparing the true market value of the monthly lifetime payments against the lump sum offered by the pension company is an indication of which option is the better way to go.

I've heard Dave Ramsey say, "You should always take the lump sum."[10] Yet, over 90 percent of the time, when I compare the monthly lifetime payments against the lump sum offered by the pension company, the monthly payments are more valuable.

Does that mean you should go with Dave Ramsey's suggestion and automatically take the lump-sum option, or go with my experience and automatically take the monthly lifetime payments?

No! It means that when you're faced with a pension decision — choosing whether you take the one-time, up-front, lump sum or monthly lifetime payments — you need to remember the principles of pension decision making and get a live, accurate market price from an annuity company. Only then can you feel confident that you are making the best pension decision for your retirement.

Then, you need to decide how to take your survivorship option.

HOW TO DECIDE WHICH PENSION SURVIVORSHIP OPTION TO TAKE

Your pension probably has a lot of different options for taking your pension. I saw one once that had seventeen different options. Today, I'm going to discuss just three.

THREE MAIN WAYS TO TAKE YOUR PENSION
AS A MONTHLY LIFETIME PAYMENT

1. **Single life annuity:** This option provides the highest monthly payment because it only covers your lifetime. You will receive this amount as long as you are alive, but when you die, payments stop completely, and your survivor receives $0. This dollar amount is very likely the dollar amount calculated by the company's pension formula.

2. **100 percent joint and survivor annuity:** This option provides the most security for your spouse but offers a lower monthly payment than a single life annuity. You receive the same payment for life, and if you pass away first, your spouse will continue receiving 100 percent of the same monthly payment for the rest of their life.

3. **50 percent joint and survivor annuity:** This option is commonly chosen as it provides a balance between the payment amount and protecting the surviving spouse. You receive a lifetime monthly payment, and if you pass away first, your spouse will receive 50 percent of this amount for the rest of their life.

There are two main problems with making the survivorship decision:

1. Taking a survivorship option, where you accept a lower monthly payment to guarantee that your surviving spouse gets something when you're gone, comes at a cost, and
2. Your monthly pension is calculated based on your life only, so that pension you've been waiting for and counting on all these years will be lower than you expected if you take any survivorship option.

I see this scenario quite often, especially with husbands, during this part of the retirement planning process. They've worked for the company for thirty years, they've done the math, and they know that they earned, for example, $200 per year of service based on the pension formula.

They know they'll be getting $6,000 for their pension, and they've plugged it into their spreadsheet and built their retirement hopes and dreams around that number.

Then they get their pension paperwork, they have to turn it in within thirty days, and they are faced with a choice:

- Take the $6,000 per month that they've been planning on for thirty years, and their wife gets $0 if they die, or
- Take a reduced amount of $5,000 per month, and their wife keeps getting $5,000 per month when they die.

Which would you choose?

If you're like most men I talk to with a pension, you're coming up with all the reasons why you can't possibly live on $1,000 less per month, but you're completely forgetting what it would be like for the other person, most likely the widow, to live on $5,000 less per month.

Yes, you should calculate and compare the value between the two options. Yes, you should consider the difference between the health of the two individuals.

Although let's be honest, most of the time, in heterosexual couples, the wife is younger and healthier and most likely going to outlive the husband.

But please, as you're making the decision on which survivorship option to take, remember that the goal of a lifetime income decision is not how to get the most money next month but how to get the most money over your lifetime — and often the way to get the most money over both of your lifetimes is to take the survivorship option.

This brings me to what seems to be the "compromise" option: 50 percent joint survivorship.

The biggest argument I hear for taking the 50 percent joint survivorship option (using my $6,000 per month example) is that you're not choosing between:

- $6,000 or $0 — that's a single life annuity.
- $5,000 or $5,000 — that's a 100 percent joint and survivor annuity.

You likely have an option that's something like:

- $5,500 or $2,750 — that's a 50 percent joint and survivor annuity. If you die first, then your spouse gets half of what you're getting.

This 50 percent option is quite tempting. There are two of you, but only one paycheck. Half the paycheck must support each of you, so if one of you is gone, then clearly, the other only needs half the pension check.

This misses the mark in that when you go from two people in a couple to one surviving spouse, the expenses don't get cut in half. Yes, your food bill will probably get cut in half. But your mortgage doesn't get cut in half. Your property taxes don't get cut in half. Your income taxes often stay the same.

I often see that when the first person dies, their expenses don't drop in half; they drop by roughly 20–30 percent.

Which might be an argument for an option I didn't mention — the 75 percent joint and survivor option that is sometimes available.

Except that pensions are not usually your only source of lifetime monthly income. If you have a pension, you probably have Social Security, too.

Unlike your pension, Social Security does not give you the option to take less money up-front so that your survivor gets more in case you die first.

Yes, there is a survivor component to Social Security, but if you are getting two Social Security checks right now, then you will lose the smaller Social Security check when the first person dies.

On average, in 2025, a couple gets $3,089 from Social Security — $1,832 from one spouse and $1,257 from the other spouse.[11]

When the first person dies, on average, you will lose 40 percent of your Social Security income!

Now, these are averages, and you should see how *your* Social Security will change when the first person dies.

But when you have Social Security dropping 40 percent already, why would you subject your surviving spouse to a pension drop of 50 percent or even 100 percent on top of that?

Yes, I do the math. Yes, I consider the options, but the fact that you cannot choose a 100 percent survivorship option with Social Security makes the ability to take a survivorship option with your pension all the more valuable.

That's why I have a bias toward taking the highest survivorship option available with pensions, and while you are doing the math on your options, you should approach the pension decision with a survivorship bias, too.

Remember, the goal for your decisions with your lifetime income plan is to make your decision based on the official name of Social Security: Old-Age and Survivors Insurance.

The one-time decisions you make with Social Security (and your pension) should be focused on:

1. Helping you in your old age
2. Helping your surviving spouse
3. Acting as insurance in case you live longer than you expect, in case inflation goes up more than you expect, in case your investments don't do as well as you expect

Now that you've figured out how to get the most income over your lifetime, let's talk about how to keep more of your hard-earned money by lowering your lifetime tax bill.

CHAPTER 8

Retirement Master Plan
⌄ STEP 3: KEEP

The third part of creating your Retirement Master Plan is figuring out how to keep more of your money by lowering your
lifetime taxes.

This third step is a good reminder that while you should
make these decisions in a particular order, each decision you
make affects other parts of your retirement.

That's why I like to describe retirement planning as a puzzle
— you're trying to fit each piece together in a way that improves
not just the one piece but every piece, every part of your retirement planning puzzle.

When you ignore the tax planning options you have in retirement, you are likely putting more of your retirement spending plan toward income taxes, which leaves less money for your
monthly lifestyle amount.

I want you to keep more of your hard-earned money, which is why you don't need just a retirement plan — you need a tax-smart retirement plan.

Now, here's what's interesting about taxes. You've probably spent a lifetime trying to lower this year's taxes, but when you hit retirement, your new goal is to try to lower your whole lifetime of taxes.

Another thing that changes with retirement is that you get a lot more flexibility to affect your tax situation each year. You probably didn't have much flexibility in your taxes when you were working. You got your W-2s and your 1099s, you gave them to your tax preparer, and you really didn't have too much ability to adjust things on your tax return.

But when you hit retirement, you have a huge amount of flexibility, and it really comes through your ability to time when your income shows up and the type of income that shows up on your tax return.

Let's talk about the timing first.

HOW YOUR WITHDRAWAL TIMING AFFECTS YOUR TAXES

What if you take money from your traditional IRA in December versus January?

That's two different tax years and could be two different tax situations.

My clients often ask me, "Should I take money out of my traditional IRA to pay off my car?"

When I make the comparison, quite often I'll see that one year has a different tax situation than the other. Perhaps they are better off taking the money out to pay off their car in December or January—it could be thousands of dollars in tax difference!

You are probably familiar with the idea of looking at different calendar tax years to try to save on your overall tax bill.

Now take that idea and extend it to before and after scenarios that don't have to do with changes in the calendar year but with changes in your own personal tax situation, such as:

- Before and after retirement
- Before and after you turn on Social Security
- Before and after you get your required minimum distributions
- Before and after one spouse dies and the other becomes the surviving spouse

If you're working with a financial advisor, they should be using software that can run thousands of scenarios to help review your before and after tax situations and discover when you are likely to be in a lower tax bracket so that you can pay taxes, on purpose, at that lower tax rate.

If you're not working with a financial advisor, it's up to you to think about and project how your tax situation will look during the different before and after points in your life.

When you're in a lower tax bracket, try to pay taxes on purpose. When you see that you'll be in a higher tax bracket, try to avoid taxable income that year.

When you're in a lower tax bracket, try to pay taxes on purpose.

Quite often, the way to pay taxes on purpose in your lower tax rate years is through Roth conversions.

HOW TO DO A ROTH CONVERSION

The key to a Roth conversion is to choose the right year and the right amount of money to convert.

Unfortunately, a few myths get in the way:

Roth Conversion Myth #1: I Can't Convert to a Roth When I'm Retired

This is not the case, although I see exactly where the confusion lies: It is true that you cannot *contribute* to a Roth IRA without any wage income, but you can *convert* to a Roth IRA any time that you want, which leads to the second myth.

Roth Conversion Myth #2: I Can't Convert to a Roth. I Have a Huge IRA, and That's Too Much in Taxes!

A lot of people think that if they have one traditional IRA, they have to convert that *entire* traditional IRA to a Roth, which is not the case.

You can convert any amount you want, even one penny, to a Roth IRA. Whatever amount you convert will just show up on that year's tax return as extra taxable income.

Wondering what the tax rate is on a Roth conversion? It's whatever tax rate that extra income shows up as. There is no special Roth conversion tax rate. The conversion amount just gets added to your other income and costs you whatever rate that extra income costs.

By this point Roth conversions probably sound so great you want to convert every year! But beware of Roth conversion myth #3:

Roth Conversion Myth #3: Roth Conversions Are Always a Good Idea

Often, people fall in love with Roth conversions, and it's easy to see why. Roth conversions promise tax-free growth to you and your beneficiaries — who wouldn't want tax-free money?

There's even a book called *The Power of Zero* by David McKnight that promises to show you how to get to a 0 percent tax rate in retirement.[12]

A 0 percent tax rate in retirement sounds great, but the question I ask is, "At what cost?"

You should only do a Roth conversion if you believe the rate at which you pay your taxes today is lower than it will be in the future.

There are lots of reasons your tax rate might actually be higher now and lower in the future, in which case, a conversion now would not make sense.

> **You should only do a Roth conversion if you believe the rate at which you pay your taxes today is lower than it will be in the future.**

One thing I come across often is that you're allowed to take money from your traditional IRA and send it straight to charity as a "qualified charitable distribution" (QCD) at a 0 percent tax rate.

If you're a charitable person, why would you convert all your traditional IRA to a Roth, pay taxes when you convert, and then later take money from your Roth IRA and give it to charity?

You would have paid taxes to get the money into the Roth, but you would have been better off instead leaving it as traditional IRA money until you were past 70½ and used the QCD rules.

I've come across several people who think that since a Roth conversion is often a good idea, it means that more of a Roth conversion is a better idea!

Unfortunately, the US tax code conspires against that thought. With the US income tax system, as your taxable income on this year's tax return grows, you move up into different, higher tax brackets.

I met Rick and Debbie a few years back. They were right at the bottom of the 24 percent tax bracket. It looked like they would always be at the bottom of the 24 percent tax bracket, which was scheduled to go up to the 28 percent rate in the future.

I recommended they convert their traditional IRA — some that year and some over the next two years — so that they could fill up the 24 percent tax bracket but not go into the next tax bracket. They would convert, over three years, roughly $540,000 within the 24 percent tax bracket, hopefully then avoiding a higher tax rate in the future.

I helped Debbie convert $180,000 early in December and called her up in January to complete the next year's conversion.

"No need," Debbie said, "I already took care of it last year."

"What do you mean?" I asked.

"Well, I figured why bother waiting to do the conversion? It can't be any different tax-wise, so let's just rip off the band-aid and Roth convert the entire account."

Unfortunately for Rick and Debbie, it did matter. Not only did that conversion all at once in December push them into the 32 percent tax bracket, but part of that conversion even got into the 35 percent tax bracket!

I calculated the difference, and I believe they paid an extra $23,000 in taxes because they converted all at once and ignored the golden rule of Roth conversions: Choose the right year and the right amount of Roth conversions.

> **The golden rule of Roth conversions: Choose the right year and the right amount of Roth conversions.**

HOW THE TYPE OF WITHDRAWAL AFFECTS YOUR TAXES

Now, it's not just the *timing* of your income withdrawals that affects your taxes; it's also the *type* of account you pull money from that matters.

There are really just four main types of accounts you can take money from in retirement. You might even have all four.

1. Traditional IRAs
2. Roth IRAs
3. Savings accounts
4. Regular brokerage accounts

Each of these accounts shows up on your tax return in a different way.

Traditional IRAs

Traditional IRAs show up on your tax return as taxable income to you during the year you withdraw the money. Generally speaking, 100 percent of what you take out is taxable.

If you take out $100,000, then $100,000 should show up as taxable to you. Now, there are exceptions such as "return of after-tax contributions" and "qualified charitable distributions (QCDs)," but we're not going to get into that here.

Taking money from your traditional IRA will have the largest tax consequence for you, so be thoughtful when you take money from your traditional account. You need to plan not just for the money you need, but also the money you might want to withhold for taxes.

If you need $50,000 out of your traditional IRA, you might also need another $20,000 on top of that just for the tax burden!

Roth IRAs

Roth IRAs are generally tax-free withdrawals to you. There are some exceptions — if you are below 59½ or haven't held the money in the account for five years — but we won't get into those here.

If you take out $100,000 from your Roth IRA in retirement, then $0 should show up as taxable to you. What's even better is that taking money from your Roth IRA does not affect any other situations, like:

- How much of your Social Security is taxable
- Your IRMAA surcharges (extra Medicare costs)
- Your ACA premium tax credit

When it comes to income taxes, taking money from your Roth IRA is the best tax situation you can find, which is why people love Roth IRAs (and often Roth conversions) so much!

Savings Accounts

When I talk about how savings accounts are taxed, I'm referring to all bank account types: checking accounts, savings accounts, money markets, and CDs. It's just easier to refer to savings accounts.

Savings accounts, when they are not part of a traditional or Roth IRA, generate interest that is taxable in the year you earn the interest.

That interest is taxable at the higher income tax rates, not capital gains rates.

That interest is taxable whether you use the money or not.

However, since the interest is already reported as taxable, you can take out your entire savings, checking, money market, or CD account and pay no tax on it!

It sounds slightly too good to be true, but it's only tax-free because you've already paid the taxes on the interest each year.

That's why, along with Roth IRAs, pulling money from your savings account is the best tax situation you can find.

Taking the money out of your savings account won't show up as taxable on your tax return, which means it won't affect any of your other tax situations.

The interest you do earn each year affects your tax return and other tax situations, which is why, if you had the choice, you would rather draw down your savings account first and use that for income or withdrawals to pay for things, and allow your Roth IRA to continue to grow.

Regular Brokerage Accounts

Your regular brokerage accounts are somewhat similar to your bank savings accounts. You pay taxes on the taxable activity that occurs, whether you use the money or not.

It's just that there's probably a lot more taxable activity going on within your regular brokerage account — that's why it's often called a "taxable account."

It's not taxable like the traditional IRA where taking money out of the account is a taxable situation. It's taxable in that all the activity going on in the account, whether you use the money or not, is likely to be reflected on your tax return.

If you have this type of account, you'll get a tax form at the end of the year that talks about all the dividends, interest, capital gains distributions, or capital gains and losses from investment sales.

The idea of capital gains, especially long-term capital gains, is where a regular, taxable brokerage account has its biggest pluses and minuses.

The minuses of a regular taxable brokerage account are that when you want to move investments around or make trades or the manager of your mutual fund wants to make trades, you have to pay taxes in the year the activity happens, not in the year that you take money out of the account. This is a negative compared to traditional IRA accounts.

A plus of the regular taxable brokerage account is that you don't have to wait until 59½ to withdraw your money, as is often the case with traditional and Roth IRAs. You can take out your money any time without a tax penalty — you'll just owe whatever taxes are due on that activity.

The biggest plus of this account is that if you hold the investment for longer than twelve months, the tax gain would be reported as a *long-term* capital gain, which is subject to lower tax rates than the rates your regular working income and your traditional IRA are subject to.

Here's an example:

- You buy a stock for $10,000.
- You hold the stock for more than twelve months and sell the stock for $20,000.
- Your gain, aka capital gain, is $10,000.
- You might have sold $20,000 in stock, you might have even spent the $20,000, but your tax reporting will show:
  - $10,000 is your tax-free cost basis, and
  - $10,000 is your long-term capital gain, subject to a lower tax rate than income taxes.

STOCK SOLD AFTER HOLDING 12+ MONTHS

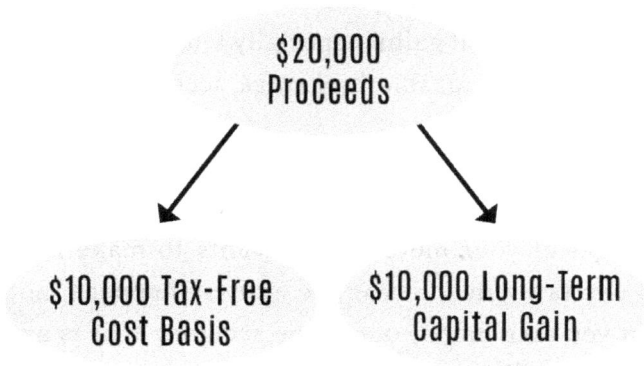

$20,000
Proceeds

$10,000 Tax-Free
Cost Basis

$10,000 Long-Term
Capital Gain

While the income tax and capital gains tax brackets used to match up perfectly, now they are slightly off, but for ease of discussion, let's pretend they match up perfectly — your tax preparer can show you the very slight differences that apply to you.

- If you're in the 0 percent, 10 percent, or 12 percent income tax bracket, your long-term capital gains rate is 0 percent.
- If you're in the 22 percent, 24 percent, 32 percent, or much of the 35 percent bracket, your long-term capital gains rate is 15 percent.
- If you're near the top of the 35 percent or in the 37 percent tax bracket, your long-term capital gains rate is 20 percent.

COMPARISON OF INCOME TAX AND CAPITAL GAINS TAX RATES

Income Tax Bracket	Long-Term Capital Gains Tax Rate
0%, 10%, or 12%	0%
22%, 24%, 32%, most of 35%	15%
Some of 35%, 37%	20%

Like I said, there is some slight mismatch as the overlap is no longer perfect, and there is also a 3.8 percent net investment income tax that applies to all investment income when you make more than $200,000 as Single and $250,000 as Married Filing Jointly, but in virtually every situation, the capital gains tax rate[13] is lower than the income tax rate.[14]

In virtually every situation, the capital gains tax rate is lower than the income tax rate.

You've learned that the *timing* of your withdrawals greatly affects your tax situation. You've learned how withdrawing from the different *types* of accounts affects your tax situation.

Hopefully, you've learned that the flexibility you have in retirement to choose the *timing* and *types* of withdrawals will allow you to project out your future tax situation, especially around the before and after parts of your financial life, so that you can pay taxes when your rates are projected to be low and avoid taxes when they look to be high, with your own tax-smart retirement plan.

Now that you've gone through and figured out how much you're likely to spend in retirement, how to maximize the amount you're making in retirement, and how to keep more of your money because you are lowering your lifetime tax bill, it's finally time to focus on the investing.

CHAPTER 9

Retirement Master Plan

📊 STEP 4: INVEST

The fourth step in creating your Retirement Master Plan is to invest your money.

You might have been thinking, "When is Jeremy going to start talking about investing? Isn't that the first thing you do for retirement planning?"

The answer, plainly, is no. Investing is not the first thing you do with retirement planning. Your investments are like fuel for your vehicle; they are important, but they are not the most important.

When you decide to drive your car somewhere, filling up with gas is important, but it's not the most important. What's most important is deciding where to go — that's like your retirement spending plan.

Next, you need to decide if you're going to take interstates or country highways. That's like your lifetime income plan. When you expect to get more income from your Social Security and pension, it's like you chose the interstate — it's a quicker, more direct route to get to where you want to go.

Then you decide which car you're going to drive to get there. Will you choose the gas-guzzler or the fuel-efficient car?

When you plan to lower your lifetime taxes through a tax-smart retirement plan, it's like you chose the fuel-efficient car. You'll get to your destination with fewer stops and less spending on gas. In the case of your retirement planning, it's spending less on taxes.

And yes, you won't get to your destination without a full tank of gas, but your other decisions were all more important. They determined your outcome a lot more than the type of fuel you put in the car.

Focusing on your investments is important, but if you don't know where you're going, how to get there, and how to make the journey more efficient, it doesn't matter how much gas or how many investments you have.

Only after you've completed the first three steps of your Retirement Master Plan should you focus on creating your retirement investment plan.

THE GOAL OF RETIREMENT INVESTING

The goal of investing in retirement is really just to fill in the gaps — the gaps that show up when your lifetime income plan isn't able to provide 100 percent of what you need for your retirement spending plan.

When you project out how much money you need, when you need it, and how much income is coming in — outside of your investments — you'll notice there are gaps where you need more money than your lifetime income can provide. That's the role of retirement investing — to fill those gaps.

And until you know those gaps, until you know when you need your money to move out of your investments and into your checking account, you really don't know how to invest your money.

HOW TO CREATE YOUR RETIREMENT INVESTMENT PLAN

The goal of your retirement investment plan is *not* to pick the best stocks and try to beat the market.

Many people try this approach and most fail. This focus is often the result of what I believe is the number one retiree mistake: trying to control what you can't control.

You can't control what the stock market does, but you can control how much risk you take within the stock market. You can control your risk through two main levers:

1. How much you keep out of the stock market through your short-term income investments, and
2. How much risk you take within the stock market, mainly through the percentage of stocks and the level of diversification you have within your long-term growth investments.

This is called the "bucket strategy."

The money you choose to set aside out of the stock market is called your income bucket.

The money you keep in the stock market for long-term growth is called your growth bucket.

BUCKET STRATEGY

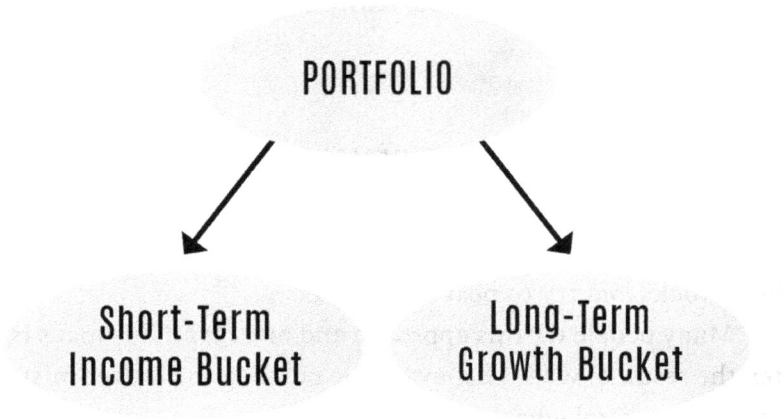

PORTFOLIO

Short-Term
Income Bucket

Long-Term
Growth Bucket

Determine How Much Money to Keep Out of the Market

If you need money next week or next month, most anyone would agree that's a short-term need that you should keep out of the market and instead invest in short-term, interest rate type investments.

But when does life switch from short-term to long-term? When do you feel comfortable investing into the market instead of setting aside the money out of the market?

Back in 2008, during the Great Financial Crisis, I was watching an interview with Warren Buffett.

The interviewer asked Buffett, "How should people invest now that the market is down?"

Warren replied with the idea that people should invest no differently than before the Great Financial Crisis. If you need money in the next five years, he suggested you put that in the bank. If you need money longer than five years from now, he suggested you put that money in the stock market.

Now, you've got to decide on your own: How long is your short-term? Is it truly five years? Is it a shorter amount of time? Is it a longer amount of time?

If you're more conservative, you would want to set aside the planned withdrawals for a longer period of time.

If you're more aggressive, you would look at your retirement investment plan and set aside the income needed for a shorter length of time into your income bucket.

Take the number of years that you consider short-term, add up the money you'll need from your investments, and that's the amount of money you ought to set aside in your income bucket.

WHAT TYPES OF INVESTMENTS DO YOU USE IN YOUR INCOME BUCKET?

- Checking accounts
- Savings accounts
- Money market accounts
- Stable value funds within your 401(k)
- Certificates of deposit (CDs)
- Short-term bond funds
- Multi-year guaranteed annuities

Really, the investments you choose for your income bucket are any investments that you can reasonably expect to return your money to you, plus interest, when you need it in the next few months or years.

If you're wondering how much money to invest for the long run in your growth bucket, the answer is simple: everything else.

If you don't need your money in the short run, then by definition, it's long-term money!

You might have thought that retirement investing involved complex financial modeling. It's really:

1. How much money do you need in the short term?
2. Set that money aside in short-term investments.
3. The rest of your money is long-term. Invest that long-term money based on the amount of ups and downs, aka volatility, you're willing to take.
4. Periodically rebalance your growth bucket to make sure you have the right level of risk for you.
5. Periodically review your retirement investment plan and move money from the growth bucket to the income bucket if you both need the money soon and the stock market is currently up.

Volatility: A measure of risk based on the frequency and level of the ups and downs you see in your investments. Most people are more concerned about the downside risk of losing money versus the upside risk of gaining more than expected.

Determine How Much Risk to Take Within the Market

Even though Warren Buffett suggested having 100 percent of your growth bucket in the stock market, you may want to take on less risk than that.

The general way you increase or decrease the risk within your growth bucket is to increase or decrease the percentage of stocks you hold. There are some other ways, like diversification and rebalancing; we'll get to those shortly.

The generally accepted average-risk portfolio has 60 percent stocks, with 40 percent bonds. You've probably heard of it before — it's called the 60/40 portfolio.

If you want more risk than average, you would take on more stocks, perhaps as much as 90–100 percent.

If you want less risk than average, then you would take on fewer stocks, perhaps as low as 20 percent or even lower.

The more risk you have, the greater potential you have for better-than-average returns, but also, the more volatility you'll see in your investments.

The less risk you have, the less potential you have for better-than-average returns, but also, the less volatility you'll see in your investments.

If you're looking for an exact answer for how much to keep in the stock market, remember it's your retirement — the right percentage of stocks is the amount that makes you comfortable, even when the market drops.

WHAT TYPES OF INVESTMENTS DO YOU USE IN YOUR GROWTH BUCKET?

- Mutual funds
- Exchange-traded funds
- Passive index funds
- Actively-managed funds
- Different types of stocks/funds:
  - Large, medium, and small
  - US and international
  - Growth, blend, and value funds
- Different types of bonds/funds
  - Medium- and long-term
  - Corporate and government bonds
  - Investment-grade and high-yield

Creating your retirement investment plan isn't a one-and-done, set-it-and-forget-it proposition. The investments will change in value on a near-daily basis for two main reasons.

1. Stocks and bonds change in value all the time. If you don't "rebalance," the risk in your growth bucket is going to change all the time. When the market goes up, you're likely to have more risk than you wanted, and when the market goes down, you're likely to have less risk (and lower return potential) than you wanted.

2. You're likely taking money out of your income bucket every month, which means the amount you have set aside for the short term is less and less each month.

Here's how you address both situations.

REBALANCE YOUR GROWTH BUCKET

Once you decide on a risk level for your growth bucket, you'll probably keep it at that level for quite some time, perhaps the rest of your life. But unless you actively rebalance your stocks and bonds, your risk level will fluctuate up and down, just like stocks and bonds fluctuate up and down!

Imagine you started with a 60/40 portfolio at the beginning of 2020. To simplify things, I'm going to assume all your stocks were in the S&P 500, and all your bonds were in the US Aggregate Bond index, with no fees and no taxes (no fees and no taxes would be pretty sweet, wouldn't it?).

If you started with $1,000,000 total, then two years later, you would have ended up with 68 percent in stocks and had more risk than you started with two years earlier, just before the S&P 500 dropped 25 percent over the next 9½ months.[15]

REBALANCE YOUR GROWTH BUCKET

	Value	Stocks	Bonds	Stock Percentage
1 Jan 2020	$1,000,000	$600,000	$400,000	60%
1 Jan 2022	$1,336,313	$913,769	$422,544	68%

Rebalancing doesn't prevent you from losing money, but it is the most commonly accepted way to make sure the risk you have in your investments is the risk level you want it to be.

And yes, some of the investing gurus reading this will accurately remember that the bond market dropped in 2022, as well, by 13 percent for the full year.

Rebalancing isn't a promise of success, but considering that the S&P 500 and the US Aggregate Bond index hadn't both dropped together since 1969,[16] if something like rebalancing worked only fifty-two out of the prior fifty-three years, I'd say that's a pretty good track record.

When it comes to your growth bucket, you'll want to set a plan for reviewing your risk, perhaps once per year, and make sure that the level of risk that you have, usually measured by the percentage of stocks that you have, matches up with the level of risk that you want.

REFILL YOUR INCOME BUCKET

Rebalancing from stocks to bonds (or perhaps bonds to stocks if the market is down) isn't the only thing you'll need to review each year.

Every year that you take money out for your retirement spending plan drops the amount of money in your income bucket.

Every year you've lived in retirement shifts your cash flow projections over one year.

Periodically, perhaps once per year, you should review your income bucket to see how much money you should hold in there.

Then review your growth bucket and determine if you want to take some profits and refill your income bucket, or perhaps if the stock market is down, like it is 30 percent of the time, you might want to leave your growth bucket alone and consider living with a little less in the income bucket, knowing you still have several years of income withdrawals set aside and allowing your growth bucket the time it needs to recover.

Here's an example. You may have decided at the start of your retirement that you need to pull $50,000 per year for the first five years from your investments. Then, starting in year six, you'll turn on your $30,000 per year Social Security, and you'll only need $20,000 per year from your income bucket.

You reach retirement and you've fully funded your income bucket with your desired amount of the next five years' expected withdrawals, which initially is $50,000 per year x 5 years = $250,000.

You lived through your first year of retirement, withdrew $50,000 as part of your plan, and have only $200,000 left in your income bucket (I assumed 0 percent interest to make the math easier).

You review your retirement spending plan and confirm that you'd like to still have the next five years of expected withdrawals in the income bucket.

But you've already lived through a year! The next five years are really years two through six in your retirement.

In the next four years, you plan to take out $50,000 per year, and in the fifth year, which is your sixth total year of retirement, you only need $20,000 because you'll be getting income from Social Security starting that year.

Notice how your cash flow needs to shift as you move through your retirement, which means the size of your income bucket shifts as well.

CASH FLOW TIMELINE

Investment Withdrawals ■ Social Security Income

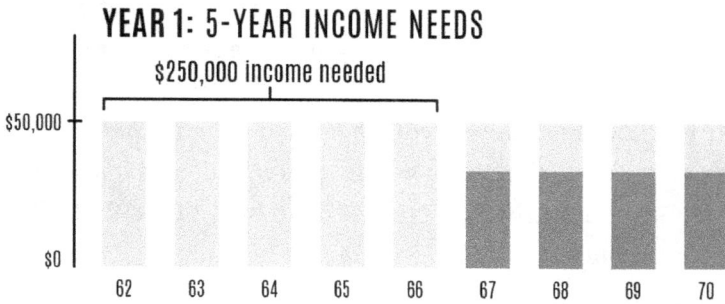

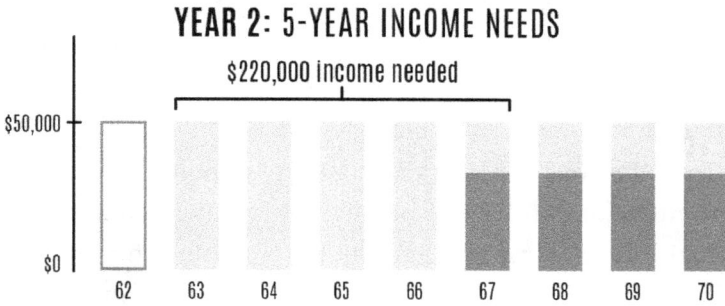

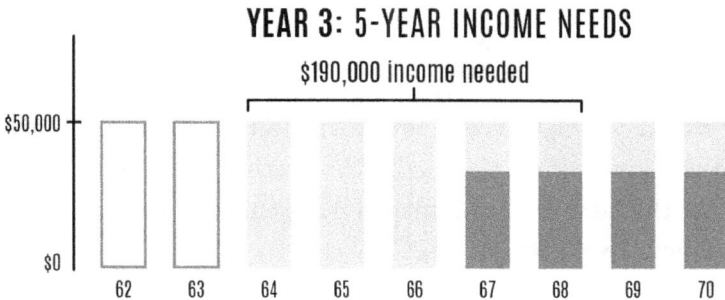

YEAR 1: 5-YEAR INCOME NEEDS

$250,000 income needed

$50,000

$0

62 63 64 65 66 67 68 69 70

YEAR 2: 5-YEAR INCOME NEEDS

$220,000 income needed

$50,000

$0

62 63 64 65 66 67 68 69 70

YEAR 3: 5-YEAR INCOME NEEDS

$190,000 income needed

$50,000

$0

62 63 64 65 66 67 68 69 70

As you complete year one of retirement and start year two, your income bucket needs $220,000 to fit your plan, and it currently has $200,000 in it.

Now, look at your growth bucket and see if you're up or down for the year.

If the market is up, you probably feel comfortable taking $20,000 from the growth bucket to refill your income bucket — except you don't have to refill it with the $50,000 you took out, just the $20,000 you expect to withdraw five years from now.

If the market is down, you've got a choice to make. Perhaps it was near an all-time high when you retired, and it's down just slightly — you might feel confident to still take $20,000 from the growth bucket to refill the income bucket.

Or perhaps the stock market is down significantly, maybe 10, 20, 30, even 50 percent!

The point of the income bucket is to help you keep your long-term growth money invested for the long term. At this point in our example, we're talking about money you're planning to take out four to five years from now.

If you believe the market is likely to be higher sometime in the next four to five years than it is now, you should feel comfortable leaving that money invested for the long term, in the growth bucket, so that it hopefully rebounds sometime in the next four to five years (which it usually does, but not always).

If you are confident the market is going to continue to go down and never get higher than it is right now over the next four to five years, then you might still refill your income bucket from your growth bucket — but know that you would be going against the 88 percent historical odds that the market recovers in the next five years.[17]

WHAT YOU CAN AND CAN'T CONTROL WITH YOUR RETIREMENT INVESTMENT PLAN

I said earlier that the number one retiree mistake is trying to control what you can't control, and you cannot control the stock market.

Neither can you control:

- The US economy
- Which politicians get elected
- Interest rates
- Inflation

But there are a few things you can control and that you ought to look at.

You can control:

- How much money you keep in the market
- How much risk you take in the market
- How well diversified you are within the market
- When you rebalance your growth bucket between stocks and bonds
- When you refill your income bucket from your growth bucket investments (hopefully at a profit)

And that doesn't include all the other things you can control, like your retirement spending plan, your lifetime income plan, and your tax-smart retirement plan.

Control what you can control.

That includes the fifth and final step in the Retirement Master Plan.

Planning for what you leave behind. We'll cover that next.

CHAPTER 10

Retirement Master Plan
∞ STEP 5: LEAVE

The fifth and final part of creating your Retirement Master Plan is focused on what you leave behind.

Sometimes you leave behind a legacy, sometimes you leave behind a mess.

I believe you'd rather avoid the mess and instead leave behind a strong legacy.

That's why you need a legacy protection plan. Your legacy is not just about the money you leave behind, or the documents you signed. Your legacy is about what happened when things didn't go as planned.

I interviewed David Edey on my podcast and he said, "Your legacy is not about *what* you leave them, but *how* you leave them."[18]

Wise words.

I often say this last step in your planning is to think of all the *risks* that might derail all your previous planning, and also to decide what to do with the *remainder* of your money when you don't need it anymore.

Or, more succinctly, "Plan for the best, prepare for the worst."

Now that you've dreamed and "planned for the best" in the first four parts of your Retirement Master Plan, let's try to prevent or lessen the effects of the big three risks to your retirement:

1. You live too long.
2. You die too soon.
3. You get too sick.

Once you've prepared for the big three retirement risks, you can focus on what remains of your investments and property so that the financial piece is a smooth transition for the people you love.

The first part of your legacy protection plan is to focus on the risks, the second part is to focus on the remainder.

LEGACY PROTECTION PLAN, PART 1: THE BIG 3 RETIREMENT RISKS

Big Retirement Risk #1: You Live Too Long

How could living too long be a retirement risk? Isn't living a long, healthy, happy retirement the goal?

Yes, it is the goal; but also, as I've heard retirement expert Moshe Milevsky often say, living longer than expected is "the great risk multiplier."

Think of all the risks that have you worried about retirement:

- Inflation
- Interest rates
- Market volatility

- Running out of money
- The cost of healthcare

The longer you live, the greater the chances these risks will get you. The longer you live, the longer the effects of high inflation, low interest rates, and high healthcare costs. The longer you live, the more likely you'll run out of money.

When you plan for retirement, don't just consider how long you might live. Also consider what happens if you live longer than expected.

And I just said, "If you live longer than expected," which sounds like it's a low-probability, *might happen* type of situation.

But no! Living longer than expected is a 50/50 proposition!

The definition of life expectancy is that half the people die before that age, and half the people make it past that age.

If you had a 50/50 chance your house was going to burn down, you would certainly plan your life and your financial matters differently.

When you plan your retirement, you need to keep in mind the very real 50/50 probability that you will live longer than expected and make decisions based on that.

You might even need to go back to steps 1–4 and adjust some of your decisions!

Again, we see that all your retirement decisions, all the big steps in your retirement planning, are like a puzzle — a puzzle with pieces that change and affect other pieces.

Your decisions on how much you spend and how you take Social Security will influence your tax situation and how your investments should look.

And your decisions now about how you prepare for the big three retirement risks ought to inform how you plan for your spending levels, your Social Security decisions, your Roth conversion and tax decisions, and how you split up your income and growth buckets.

If you're concerned about this 50/50 probability retirement risk, then some steps you could take are:

- Delay Social Security so that you have a higher monthly payment that lasts as long as you do.
- Take your pension as a monthly payment instead of a lump-sum, one-time payment.
- You might even be able to delay taking your pension, much like Social Security, so that you get a higher monthly payment that lasts as long as you do.

Big Retirement Risk #2: You Die Too Soon

Now that you've prepared for the very real 50/50 chance that you'll live longer than expected, it's time to prepare for the very real 50/50 chance that you won't live as long as you expected.

As you make your spending decisions, as well as your Social Security, pension, and tax decisions, consider what would happen if you didn't live to your life expectancy.

It's not fun to think about, but it's a strong possibility — it happens half the time!

Do you want to make decisions that leave your spouse unprepared?

Do you want to wait until later to take that trip of a lifetime, when later might never arrive?

When You Create Your Retirement Spending Plan, Consider Using a Vacation Bucket, Not a Travel Budget

I'm not sure where I heard it first, but I think it's a genius idea. Instead of planning for $5,000/year in travel over the next thirty years in your budget, set aside $150,000 (the same dollar amount) into your vacation bucket. Then, try to spend down your vacation bucket over the first five, ten, or fifteen years of your retirement.

- You're more likely to be healthier in the first part of your retirement and more likely to be able to take the types of trips you'd like to do.
- Statistically, you're more likely to be around in the first part of retirement, so you're more likely to enjoy those vacations.
- And, if you happen to live to an average or above average age and you used up your vacation bucket early on, that's OK. You can remember the good times from the vacations you had and experience what the author of *Die With Zero*, Bill Perkins, calls "memory dividends."[19]

When You Create Your Lifetime Income Plan, Consider How Your Choices Affect Your Surviving Spouse

Deciding how and when to take your Social Security and pension is tough.

You've worked for thirty-five-plus years and paid into your Social Security, and you can't wait to have Social Security start paying back to you. Then, some financial advisor or retirement guru says you should wait a little longer! Don't they realize you've waited long enough? It's time to get paid!

Or maybe you have a pension, and every year you've worked there, you get a piece of paper showing you exactly how much you'll get in a monthly pension at your retirement age. Then you hit retirement, and they give you another piece of paper with all the different options, and every single one that has "survivorship" associated with it shows you getting much less in retirement, maybe even 20 percent less than the amount you were planning on.

Don't they realize you've planned your retirement based on getting 100 percent of your pension, not 80 percent of your promised amount?

I get it. It's tough to retire today and not get Social Security right away. It's tough to retire today and get less pension income than you planned for.

But retirement planning isn't about getting the most money today. It's about getting the most money over your lifetime, and a big risk to your retirement planning is that, when you're in a couple, one of you doesn't get the lifetime that you expected, but the other one still does.

When you plan your Social Security and when you decide on your pension, don't just consider, "How do *I* get the most out of this?" Consider "How do *we* get the most out of this?" and especially, "How does the surviving spouse get the most out of this?"

And let's be honest here. This is typically a situation where the husband has a higher Social Security or pension and has to make a decision on when and how he takes his Social Security or pension.

The average Social Security check for a male is 25 percent higher than that of a female.[20]

78 percent of surviving spouses in a couple are female.[21]

Quite often, the 90-year-old widow is living on the income decisions made thirty years earlier by her now-deceased husband.

Before you sign the paperwork for your Social Security and your pension, take some time and consider what that income will look like for the surviving spouse.

Who knows, that surviving spouse might even be you!

Big Retirement Risk #3: You Get Too Sick

When you retire, there are two big health costs to consider.

1. Your regular doctor and hospital health costs that you're somewhat used to already. Once you hit 65, these are mainly covered by Medicare.
2. The long-term care costs that occur when you can't take care of yourself the way you used to. These costs are *not* covered by Medicare.

What's interesting about healthcare costs in retirement is that the longer you live, usually your health decreases, and your healthcare costs increase.

While many people go into retirement worried about the cost of healthcare, they often don't plan for three significant factors:

1. Your healthcare costs aren't a flat budget line item throughout your retirement. Your annual costs are expected to double between the ages of 70 and 90.[22]
2. You can't plan for the averages. You can find numbers for average healthcare spending, but the averages aren't that useful. In one study, the top 10 percent of the healthcare spenders accounted for 52 percent of the healthcare costs, mostly through the cost of nursing homes.[23]
3. Your decisions on how to pay for the increasing costs of regular medical spending and how to pay for the potential of high nursing home costs are largely set in stone by the time you turn 65.

Imagine that one day, your refrigerator stops working. What do you do? You take money out of your savings or your income and buy a new one. And while you have choices on which refrigerator to buy, when you go to buy a new refrigerator, you'll pay the same price as everyone else. You won't pay ten times the price as someone else because of a decision you made years ago.

Healthcare doesn't work the way refrigerator buying does. When you're past 65 and need healthcare, you can't just buy the health insurance plan that fits you best right now.

You're often stuck in the choice you made years earlier on whether you preferred Original Medicare with a Medigap policy or Medicare Advantage. You might even be part of the 9 percent of those age 65-plus who chose not to have any insurance beyond Medicare at all.[24]

Imagine if the price of the refrigerator you buy at 75 is dictated by a choice you made at 65.

What if you're part of the unlucky 10 percent who account for half of medical spending in the US? It's probably because you're in a nursing home.

And your choice of whether you pay those nursing home costs or insurance pays those costs was made by you years earlier, often before you even hit retirement age.

Again, imagine if the price of the refrigerator you buy at 90 is dictated by a choice you made at 65!

That's how health insurance works in this country — you have to make choices years and years ahead of time that affect how your healthcare works and how much it costs down the road.

These are often one-time choices of whether you have long-term care insurance or not, whether you chose Original Medicare with a Medigap plan or not.

With healthcare costs doubling between ages 70 and 90, and a small percentage of the unlucky few paying the majority of the healthcare costs, how you prepare for retirement risk number three as you approach retirement will dictate a lot of how your retirement goes.

There are whole books written on the Medicare decisions you face at 65. I've done several podcast episodes and YouTube video series on those choices. Those resources are available at JeremyKeil.com.

Your Medicare choices are important, and every retiree must face them. But whether you're thinking about Medicare or long-term care, remember: your decisions today don't just affect you now. They impact the rest of your retirement.

When making these choices, don't focus only on what works best for you today. Instead, think about what's best for your future, because some decisions can't be changed later. Consider not just yourself today, but also your spouse and even your kids down the road. How will these choices affect you and your family twenty-five to thirty years from now?

For now, let's focus on one of the biggest potential costs in retirement: long-term care. While you may end up never needing it, planning for it is essential.

YOU NEED A LONG-TERM CARE PLAN

When you hear the phrase long-term care, especially coming from a financial advisor, you probably immediately think of long-term care insurance (LTCI).

That could be part of it, but that's not what I'm talking about right now. Here's what I believe about long-term care (insurance):

Not everyone needs long-term care insurance, but everyone needs a long-term care plan.

Your long-term care plan boils down to three key decisions:

> Not everyone needs long-term care insurance, but everyone needs a long-term care plan.

1. Where do you want the care to take place?
2. Who is going to take care of you?
3. How are you going to pay for the care?

Where Do You Want Your Care to Take Place?

The "where" part of your long-term care might have to do with geography — where you want to live — or the type of housing you prefer.

I have one client who retired and wanted to move halfway between their two kids, roughly two hours from each of them — and, more importantly, the grandkids! Their son told them they are better off living near one or the other kid so that when they get older, they'll have one of them just down the road instead of both of them several hours away.

I have other clients who chose a continuing care retirement community (CCRC), which offers independent living, assisted living, and skilled nursing care all in one location. They thought through where they want to receive their future long-term care, and they made sure that their housing choices in their early 70s supported their care needs fifteen to twenty years down the road.

Most people I talk to say, "I don't want to leave my home," but without planning for that possibility, that statement is really just a wish. I've had clients who didn't want to leave their home, but when the husband needed a wheelchair, they reluctantly moved him to assisted living. Instead, they could have had him stay at home for at least another year if they had just planned out and renovated their bathroom ahead of time.

I've seen others proactively get their home ready, renovating their showers and doorways to be zero-entry while in their early 60s, so they could stay in their home, hopefully into their 90s!

Who Is Going to Take Care of You?

Years ago, older family members often moved into their relatives' homes so that the younger generation could take care of them. You might have grown up with a grandparent living in your home. But today, the expectations aren't so clear.

- Are your parents expecting to move in with you?
- Do you expect your kids to take care of you when you're older? If so, have you told them that?

It's nice when families take care of each other. It's perfectly OK, too, if they choose not to provide daily healthcare for each other. But what's better, in either situation, is to think through what you'd like and to communicate your thoughts with the people it's going to affect.

I know a widower who is spending three months out of the year with each of his four kids. It seems to be working well now, but I wonder what will happen when he gets older, and he can't move around the country so much. Which one of his kids will he be living near when that time comes?

I have a client whose only child lives two hours away from him. He was telling me that since his son and daughter-in-law have their own kids to worry about, he didn't want to be a burden to his son or interrupt their family life.

Together, we came up with a good solution for him. My client bought the absolute minimum value long-term care insurance policy, not so much for the insurance coverage, but because the insurance company provides a "care coordinator" who will be able to assist my client and his son in finding the best healthcare or living facilities when, and if, he needs long-term care.

That way, my client and his son can feel good that Dad is getting the best care — without his son needing to travel two hours away and quickly become experts in the world of Milwaukee long-term care and health facilities.

How Are You Going to Pay For the Care?

There are three basic ways long-term care is paid for in the US:

1. The government, through Medicaid, aka Title 19
2. Out of your own pocket, through your investments and income
3. Long-term care insurance

Notice how I didn't say Medicare. Medicare does *not* cover long-term care. You will need to pay the cost on your own, through your insurance, or perhaps through a different program called Medicaid, that's designed for people with limited income and resources.

Here's what Medicare has to say: "**Medicare and most other health insurance, including Medicare Supplement Insurance (Medigap), don't pay for non-medical long-term care.**"[25]

I kept that in bold because Medicare puts it in bold on their website!

If the government is paying for your long-term care, it's likely through Medicaid.

As an example, to qualify for Medicaid in Wisconsin:

- When you're a couple, the non-institutionalized spouse is allowed to keep $157,920, one house, and one car.[26]
- When you're single, you're allowed to keep $2,000.[27]

If you're reading this book, and you've saved well within your 401(k) and other investments, it's hard to imagine that the cost of your care will be so large that you'll spend down your assets all the way to the point where you qualify for Medicaid.

It's a possibility, but it's usually *not* the first choice. The first choice usually comes down to a question I get all the time: "Should I self-insure or buy long-term care insurance?"

Should I Self-Insure or Buy Long-Term Care Insurance?

Before we talk about the difference between self-insurance and buying long-term care insurance, I need to share a pet peeve of mine.

The phrase "self-insurance."

Self-insurance doesn't exist. Self-insurance is impossible.

Insurance works by spreading the risk of a potential cost across a lot of people. Instead of facing an unpredictable, potentially large cost, you pay a fixed, predictable amount — your insurance premium — to protect yourself from financial uncertainty.

No one, ever, anywhere, has ever self-insured against anything.

Now, you can "self-fund." You can choose not to buy insurance. But that's not self-insurance — that's choosing not to insure.

So, from here on out, I'll refer to "self-insurance" as "self-funding." OK. Rant over. Thank you for hearing me out.

Here's the deal with self-funding versus buying insurance.

You'll never find a math solution to the question, "Should I self-fund or buy long-term care insurance?"

Long-term care insurance is a competitive marketplace with smart actuary, investment, and finance people making sure the premiums are fair.

Buying long-term care insurance is a fair deal if you buy it, which also means it's a fair deal to not buy it. Which means there's no math answer to this problem. Here's the best answer I can give you:

- Long-term care insurance is a better deal if you use it.
- Self-funding is a better deal if you don't use it.

The problem is you don't know which way things will go — whether you'll use it or not.

Here's how I suggest you solve the dilemma of whether to buy insurance or not.

- Imagine needing long-term care and not having insurance. How does that feel?
- Imagine paying premiums for years and never using it. How does that feel?

Which scenario bothers you more?

- If not having insurance worries you more, you may want to buy it.
- If paying for insurance you might not use bothers you more, you may want to self-fund.

And if you self-fund, I suggest you don't just *hope* that you never need the care; I suggest you make use of the idea that Morningstar's retirement expert, Christine Benz, shares as her preferred long-term care planning method — a long-term care fund.[28]

In Christine's book, *How to Retire*, she suggests you set aside a specific amount of money in a specific account for your future long-term care needs, and then you exclude that account from your retirement income planning.[29]

Instead of having $1.2 million in investments that you plug into your retirement planning, perhaps hold $200,000 in reserve as your "long-term care fund" and only put the remaining $1 million in investments into your retirement income projections.

If you need long-term care later on, then you'll feel confident you have a large chunk of money set aside to pay for it.

If you don't need the long-term care, you'll be glad you didn't pay premiums along the way, and you'll have more money available to help the surviving spouse in the future or leave a larger inheritance for the kids.

My Perspective on Self-Funding vs. Buying Insurance

I've said that buying long-term care insurance is not a better financial deal than self-funding. But I have seen it lead to better outcomes.

Notice how your parents are dealing with these issues. Now imagine a time when you're older. Your doctor says you need some extra help, and the kids are encouraging you to get the extra help.

If you have to spend your own money to pay for the extra help, are you willing to do that?

Or imagine you've been paying premiums into your long-term care insurance for years. When your doctor says, "It's time to start paying for the extra care you need," you're far more likely to accept the help you need when you need it when you know the insurance company is going to help you pay for that care.

Now you're faced with your decision: will you self-fund, or will you buy insurance?

The answer to that question isn't nearly as important as the fact that you've asked yourself that question, you've thought it through, and you've created a plan for when you need long-term care.

AFTER YOU PLAN FOR THE BIG 3 RETIREMENT RISKS

Now, hopefully, everything works out. You planned for and experienced the retirement you wanted. You prepared for the big three retirement risks, and things worked out. You've probably got some money left over that you'll be leaving behind.

That's where your estate planning comes in. It's the final, highly important piece in creating your Retirement Master Plan.

LEGACY PROTECTION PLAN, PART 2: ESTATE PLANNING

It certainly isn't fun to plan out your estate because who wants to think about the time when you're no longer living? But a good, complete Retirement Master Plan includes planning not just for when your retirement begins but also when your retirement ends.

Now, you may think estate planning only involves getting money to your kids when you die, but it really includes a lot of decisions that occur while you're alive and that affect you and your spouse before someone else inherits the money.

The two main goals of estate planning are to protect you and your spouse in case bad things happen in an untimely manner, like an early death or an extra-long-term health situation, and to make your inheritance as easy and tax-efficient as possible for the people and charities you care about.

Estate Planning Goal #1: Protect Yourself and Your Spouse in Case Bad Things Happen

While I talked earlier about the planning decisions you need to make to prepare for the big three retirement risks, it's time to focus on, as David Edey said, "not *what* you leave them, but *how* you leave them."

And how you leave your family has a lot to do with the documents you put in place ahead of time.

These documents don't talk just about what happens when you die but also about what happens if you're still living and can't make decisions for yourself.

Perhaps you've had an accident. Perhaps you're in the hospital having surgery, and the recovery is taking longer than expected. Perhaps your mental abilities are on a long, slow decline. You're still living, but someone else will need to make healthcare and financial decisions for you.

When you take care of your basic estate planning, you will create and sign several documents that address different things, depending on whether you're still living or have passed on.

BASIC ESTATE PLANNING DOCUMENTS WHEN YOU'RE ALIVE

To protect your spouse and yourself and to make life easier for the people who will be helping you while you are still living, your estate planning may include some or all of these documents:

- Healthcare power of attorney
- Financial power of attorney
- Marital property agreement
- Healthcare directive/living will

Healthcare Power of Attorney

A healthcare power of attorney document helps your family make healthcare decisions when you can't. Maybe you're in surgery and something happened, and the doctor needs you to choose between option A or B. Well, you can't make that choice because you're under anesthesia; that's when your healthcare agent steps in, authorized by you through your power of attorney document.

When you set up your healthcare power of attorney, you will choose your healthcare agent, your alternate healthcare agent if the first one is unable or unwilling to act, and get two witnesses to sign.

Most importantly, you should tell your agent and alternate healthcare agent that they have this responsibility, give them a copy of your healthcare power of attorney document, and share with them your thoughts and beliefs about medical treatment.

This is important stuff, and these healthcare agents are important people, because theoretically, you might be giving them the power to pull the plug!

Financial Power of Attorney

This document allows someone you choose to make all the financial decisions that you would normally make yourself — that is, as long as you give them the power to make those decisions!

When you fill out the financial power of attorney, you will write down who is your financial agent, who will become the successor agent if the first one is unable or unwilling to act, and which types of financial decisions they can make, for example, decisions about buying, holding, or selling your real property (like your house and car) or moving money around within bank accounts, stocks and bonds, and retirement accounts. Even decisions like paying taxes or giving money to charity or to your kids.

You might also limit the power of attorney; for example, you could write down: "Never sell my house or my baseball card collection."

Then, you'll sign it in front of a notary and have them notarize it, and it's often good to have your financial agent sign the document as well, accepting their duties as your financial agent.

POA VS. AGENT

Most people refer to the person who makes decisions when they are no longer able to as their POA, which is short for power of attorney. Technically, though, this person is their agent. The power of attorney (POA) is the document that spells out who your agent is and what powers they have and gives the agent the legal authority to act on your behalf, whether it's for healthcare or finances.

Marital Property Agreement

A marital property agreement is used to write down how property will be divided between two married people in the event of a divorce or death. This is especially important in community property states like the one I live in, Wisconsin.

It's also used to help avoid probate for your surviving spouse. Perhaps you have a piece of property or some sort of investment that is currently in your name only, perhaps one you inherited. You can use a marital property agreement to specify whether or not your spouse has any rights to this property or investment when you pass.

If you give them those rights, then when you die, your spouse can use the marital property agreement to transfer the property or investment into their name without going through the probate system.

Healthcare Directive/Living Will

Quite often, your lawyer will ask you to create a healthcare directive, otherwise known as a living will, or sometimes as a "declaration to physicians."

These documents typically include your thoughts about feeding tubes, life support, going to a nursing home, and whether you want your organs donated.

This document may or may not be necessary, depending on the state you live in and how your lawyer sets up your healthcare power of attorney document.

The lawyer I recommend most often in Wisconsin doesn't like the idea of healthcare directives, especially the ones provided by your doctor or hospital. She has a couple of reasons:

1. The healthcare directive/living will might conflict with the healthcare power of attorney document, and that creates issues. Instead, she recommends including these types of directives within the healthcare power of attorney.

2. The healthcare directive provided by your doctor or hospital might be set up to make the doctor or hospital's lives easier, not necessarily to match the wishes you have, *and*, more importantly, is often given to you to sign by someone with no legal training who can't properly answer your legal questions.

Meanwhile, the lawyer I most often recommend in Illinois likes the idea of a healthcare directive/living will. He believes that the two different documents serve two different purposes (naming your healthcare agent and expressing your end-of-life wishes) and that they complement each other.

I'm not going to tell you which way you need to go, but it highlights a few things:

1. Estate planning may be state-specific, so it's good to find a lawyer within your state who focuses on estate planning as their main area of legal practice.

2. Whether your lawyer suggests having a healthcare directive or not, or having a trust, you should ask why they recommend certain things and how these recommendations benefit you and your family.

ESTATE PLANNING GOAL #2: MAKE YOUR INHERITANCE AS EASY AND TAX-EFFICIENT AS POSSIBLE

Often, retirees will leave money behind to the people or places they care about. But to be a true retirement master, you will want to ensure your inheritance gets to the people and charities you care about as easily and as tax-efficiently as possible.

You might think that this part is focused on deciding if you should have a will or a trust, but keep in mind that oftentimes, most of your money doesn't even go through the will or trust; it probably gets sent out through something called beneficiaries.

If you think that your will takes care of your 401(k), traditional IRA, Roth IRA, brokerage accounts, life insurance, or mutual funds, think again. Most of these can be set up to pay out to your beneficiaries just by filling out a simple form directly with the financial institution.

Make sure that these investment accounts have a beneficiary form on file that tells the financial company how to send this money out when you die.

Basic Estate Planning Documents When You're No Longer Alive

Wills

The will declares what you want to happen with your estate.

The will is important, especially if you have minor children, because you can use that to spell out who is going to become their guardian.

A key component of the will is naming your executor, aka personal representative. This is the person in charge of making sure your money and things go out to the people you name in the will. Your executor is often the same person you named as your financial agent in your power of attorney, but not necessarily.

THE DIFFERENCE BETWEEN FINANCIAL POA AND EXECUTOR

The number one complaint I hear from lawyers, insurance agents, and financial advisors related to financial powers of attorney is when your financial agent calls in and says, "I'm Mom's financial power of attorney. She died, and I need to do certain things with her accounts." Why do financial professionals complain when this happens?

It's because the financial power of attorney ends at death — it's not valid anymore. Remember that the power of attorney is to give authority to someone who makes financial decisions on your behalf. When you die, you can't give authority to anyone, and there's no more "on your behalf" — now we're talking wills and trusts, and it's the executor of the will or the trustee of the trust who has the power.

That might be the same *person* as the financial agent in your financial power of attorney — but when you die, it's a different *document* that's in charge of your money.

Wills are important. They are often an easy way to spell out how you want your money and things to be distributed. They are usually shorter and simpler to create than a trust; perhaps that's why they are often called a simple will.

But with that simplicity comes a word that most people fear and want to avoid: probate.

Probate is the part of the court system that records your will and certifies that the money went out to whom it was supposed to. When you involve the court system, the whole process often takes longer than you want. It often brings lawyers into the mix, and the legal fees become larger than you want.

But if you don't like the idea of probate — a long, expensive process for your family to go through after you die — then imagine what it would look like, how long things would take, and how expensive it might become if you don't have a will!

If you don't have a will when you die, it's called intestacy. Your stuff will go through probate; you didn't avoid that, but now your money and stuff are divided out based on your state's intestacy laws. Imagine how much longer and more expensive it might be if the court system has to figure out who is related to you instead of having a simple will that tells them where you want your money to go.

Often, people who have saved up an average or above-average amount of money want to avoid probate and all that comes with it.

In that case, they often create a trust as their main estate planning document. A trust dictates where your money is supposed to go, just like a will, but it doesn't need the probate court system to make it happen.

Trusts

A lot of people ask me about trusts and if a trust is right for them.

I believe a trust makes sense when you have any of these situations:

- You want to add some restrictions or requirements, such as wanting your inheritance to be used for education or to restrict your kids from getting money in a way that could harm them, for example, in cases of potential drug/alcohol abuse or divorce.
- You want to get money to a family member with special needs, but make sure they are still eligible for government assistance.
- You own property, such as a house or cabin, especially if there is more than one beneficiary or if it is out of state.
- You want to avoid probate and keep your family's financial matters away from the probate court.

People often tell me they want a trust so they can avoid estate tax or inheritance tax. Well, I have good news and bad news for you.

The bad news is that the standard trust your lawyer prepares, known as a revocable living trust, will do absolutely nothing to save you and your family estate or inheritance tax. Any money or property you have in your revocable living trust will still be a part of your estate; it will still be subject to estate tax and inheritance tax.

Now for the good news. In 2025, an individual needs to leave behind over $13.99 million for there to be an estate tax.[30] This is roughly 0.1 percent of all estate situations.

There are still twelve states, along with Washington, DC, that have their own estate tax,[31] so make sure you find out whether your state has an inheritance or estate tax and if it applies to your situation.

There hasn't been an inheritance tax in Wisconsin, where I live, since 1992, but as of the end of 2024, there are still six states with inheritance taxes.

Focusing on the federal estate tax, since that could affect all Americans, with an estate needing to be $14 million for one person or $28 million for a couple, the inheritance and estate taxes are probably something you don't need to worry about, but income tax very well could be.

THE REAL DEATH TAX YOU SHOULD PLAN FOR

While many people are concerned about estate and inheritance taxes upon their passing, very few reach the level where those taxes come into play. Meanwhile, almost every retiree I work with owns traditional retirement accounts. When you die, the people who inherit these accounts will have to pay *regular income taxes* on the amount of money that you've never paid taxes on before. Yes, if it's your spouse who inherits your accounts, they won't owe taxes right away, but chances are those accounts will eventually be inherited by somebody.

Many people ignore in their planning that these accounts will eventually become taxable. I've seen tax costs of $100,000 or more. If you're trying to become a true retirement master, when you do your retirement planning, make sure to project out how much of your traditional retirement accounts will be passed on to the next generation. Consider different ways to lower the overall tax bill paid by you and your beneficiaries, such as Roth conversions or leaving your tax-free money to people and your taxable money to charity.

While there are many different kinds of trusts and different reasons to get a trust, such as when your estate is larger than $14 or $28 million, I'm going to focus on the standard trust that you are likely to have prepared: the revocable living trust.

Revocable Living Trusts

A revocable living trust is a legal document that spells out how you'd like your money and property to be distributed when you die. It's really not much different than a will, except that a will needs to go through probate to accomplish your wishes, and a trust does not.

To fully understand the revocable living trust, you need to understand each of the three words.

Revocable means you can change it or get rid of it at any time.

Living means it was created while you're alive and is in effect while you're alive. Meanwhile, a will has no power until you die.

Trust means it's an entity with rules. There are people in charge, called trustees, and people who benefit, called beneficiaries.

When you create the revocable living trust, you are called the grantor. You get to decide who is in charge of the trust, the trustee.

You are often the trustee of the trust while you're living, and you name another trustee, often a person, but it could also be a corporate trustee — a trust company or other financial institution — to be in charge after you die.

The people or charities who benefit from the trust are called beneficiaries. These are most often you and your spouse, if you have one, while you're living, and your kids, relatives, and favorite charities after your passing.

Because you can change the trust anytime while you are alive, and you are most often the person in charge of the trust and who benefits from the trust, the income from the trust will show up on your tax return, and the value of the trust is included in your estate.

While you're living, your trust doesn't need its own tax ID number and doesn't file its own tax return.

A revocable living trust does not help reduce your income taxes, gift taxes, or estate taxes. Really, there is no tax benefit at all.

Despite a standard trust not helping with estate taxes, when you own property or have more than perhaps $50,000, you often want a trust to dictate how your money is divided.

If you're wondering about the benefits of a trust, just remember the three P's of trust planning: privacy, protection, and probate.

1. Privacy: Trusts are private documents and are not public records, unlike wills. No one should be able to see your trust who you don't want to see your trust.
2. Protection: A trust is a much more effective document than a will for setting up the protections described above.
3. Probate: A trust is settled outside of the court system, so any money passed through the trust should be settled far quicker and less expensively than if that money were passed through a will, which goes through probate.

Why You Often Have a Trust *and* a Will

When you ask an estate lawyer, "Which do I need, a trust or a will?" they are likely to give you an answer that surprises you. They are likely to say:

"You need a trust *and* a will."

Estate planning isn't about the either/or of trust versus will. You've already learned that it includes seemingly non-estate documents like powers of attorney and healthcare directives.

And if you go through and decide that a trust-based estate plan is right for you, then you are very likely to get both a trust and a will.

The trust is there to provide the three P's of trust planning: privacy, protection, and probate avoidance.

You'll still get a will, though, from your trust-based estate plan. Your lawyer might call it a "pour-over will" or a "backup will" instead of a "simple will." Really, they're not much different other than what they call it, which gives an indication of why you still need a will when you get a trust.

You still need a will because if anything happens to not already be named in your trust or directed toward your trust upon your passing, then that asset or property will go through the will and "pour over" into your trust. The will is there as a "backup" in case you didn't get things into your trust in time.

You'd rather have a will that says: "All my stuff goes to my trust," than have any of your assets or property miss the trust somehow, and then you have to go to probate anyway.

That's why you need a will, even if you choose to get a trust.

But with all this planning and all your decisions about your estate, your trust and your will might not be the most important documents you have. Most retirees have the majority of their money in retirement accounts, brokerage accounts, and life insurance, and all of those will pass on not to the people you have listed in your trust or will but to the people you have listed in your beneficiary forms.

Most of Your Money Won't Even Be in Your Trust or Go Through Your Will

Most retirees I talk to hold the vast majority of their assets in their retirement accounts like traditional IRAs, Roth IRAs, and 401(k)s. Some of them have significant investments in brokerage accounts. Many of them have life insurance that they plan to pass on. Almost all of them own their own home.

And for every single account I just mentioned, the most important piece of estate planning paperwork is not a trust or a will — it is a beneficiary form.

When you open an account like an IRA or 401(k), one of the forms you sign is a beneficiary form. This is part of your account contract, and whatever you list on the beneficiary form is how things will pay out.

Your will or trust will take care of whatever money flows through the will or trust. But in the world of retirement savers, most of your money will be paid out through the beneficiary forms you have on file for your accounts.

If you thought having a will would take care of your inheritance, think again. After you create your inheritance plan in your will or trust, you'll need to update your beneficiary forms to coordinate with your will or trust.

Did you set up a trust with trustees and restrictions and provisions? Unless money goes through the trust, that money doesn't have to follow the rules of the trust that you took all this time to think about and create.

Even your house and bank accounts can be inherited through a beneficiary form. When you create a trust, you might retitle your house and bank account in the name of the trust, or you might set up a "transfer on death" form that keeps the house or account in your name but lists out the beneficiaries, which could be your trust, for when you die.

There are countless stories about people who die, who maybe had a trust or will but whose beneficiary forms on old accounts left money to ex-spouses or other people they no longer wanted to leave money to.

Before you leave your estate planning lawyer's office, make sure they give you a listing of exactly how to set up your beneficiaries on your IRAs, 401(k)s, brokerage, and other accounts. Then go actually update your beneficiary forms.

It just might be the most important estate planning paperwork you fill out.

Estate planning usually isn't on the top of your list for a fun activity, but it certainly is important for responsible people to plan out how they will take care of themselves, their spouse, their family, and the charities they care about.

Now that you've gone through and finished your estate planning, you might have thought you were finished creating your Retirement Master Plan. You thought you reached the end, but it's time to go back to the beginning to discover the most important number you need, before you even start step 1 of your Retirement Master Plan.

CHAPTER 11

The Most Important Number

Now that you've learned the five simple steps to take in creating your Retirement Master Plan, you're probably wondering where to start. It makes sense to start at step 1: Spend.

It makes sense to start thinking about your retirement budget and how much you'll need every month for the rest of your life, but there are two parts to the retirement spending equation.

1. How *much* you are going to spend in retirement
2. How *long* you are going to spend in retirement

Unfortunately, both parts of that equation are difficult to figure out, which is why Nobel Prize-winning economist William Sharpe calls the retirement income puzzle the "nastiest, hardest problem in finance."[32]

It's not a simple, "I need $50,000 per year for twenty years, so I need $1 million." You've got to account for interest rates, stock market fluctuations, the change in your spending patterns, taxes, tax changes, and inflation, as well as how long you might live.

It's a difficult problem, but you've probably spent a lot more time thinking about the first part of the equation (how much) than you have thinking about the second part (how long). And it's the second part, how long you are going to spend in retirement, that is the biggest driver of your retirement spending plan.

It's important, not only because it's a part of your retirement spending plan, but also because getting to this number, and how you view it, will help you make better decisions with your Social Security, your Medicare, your tax planning, your investments, and virtually every other retirement decision you'll face.

Your retirement longevity number is the number one, most important number in your Retirement Master Plan, yet up until this moment, you probably haven't thought about it much. You probably have the wrong number in mind, and you probably haven't been taught how to discover your retirement longevity number.

But by the end of this chapter, you'll know exactly how to discover this number and how to think about it.

At the end of this chapter, I'm going to ask you to put down this book and go to a website so that you can discover your retirement longevity number today.

It's the first step of the first step, and it will only take you five minutes.

THE RETIREMENT LONGEVITY NUMBER YOU HAVE IN MIND RIGHT NOW IS PROBABLY WRONG

I hate telling someone they are wrong. It's not fun to begin with, but when you're asking someone to make a change or to take a step, especially with something as important and emotional as money, telling someone they are wrong is hardly ever helpful. But right now, I have to do it.

Now, take just a second and think of how long you are likely to live, what's commonly known as your life expectancy.

Do you have an age in mind?

Excellent.

Now I hate to do this; you know I hate to do this ...

But your number is probably wrong.

Sorry. I had to do it, but it's for your own good. And it's not your fault, really.

Before I show you why virtually everything you've been told about life expectancy is wrong, I need to explain why I'm using the term "retirement longevity number" and not "life expectancy."

I'm using "retirement longevity number" because there are two key parts of retirement:

1. When your retirement starts
2. When your retirement ends

If you focus on "life expectancy," you're only focused on one key part of the number. You really need to get a clearer picture of the end of your retirement *and* the start of your retirement, which is why I think a true retirement master focuses on the retirement longevity number.

We'll talk about the start of your retirement later on in this chapter, but first, let's talk about the end of your retirement — your life expectancy.

WHY EVERYTHING YOU'VE BEEN TOLD ABOUT YOUR LIFE EXPECTANCY IS WRONG

Once or twice a year, you'll see news stories talking about life expectancy in America, and whether it's higher or lower. It's hard to escape the stories, and it's even harder to escape the one number they publish, probably around age 78.

It's a number that gets implanted into your brain. It's a number that affects your decisions about when to retire, when to take Social Security, when to take your pension, and which survivorship option to take with your pension.

And it's a number that's just plain irrelevant when you're trying to plan for retirement.

The next time you read an article talking about life expectancy in America, pay special attention to the full phrase, which is "life expectancy at birth."[33] This is not *your* life expectancy; this is the life expectancy of someone just born, not someone who is about to retire.

Think of it this way: if you're trying to retire today, you weren't born yesterday.

What you need to dive into is not life expectancy at birth, but the life expectancy at your current age. Better yet, you need your own personalized life expectancy, which I'm going to show you how to get.

Before we get into your own personalized life expectancy, let's look at some better data that you won't find in the news articles. You'll have to go directly to the source, the CDC, to see this data.[34]

When you dig into the CDC data, yes, you'll see that "life expectancy at birth" was 78.4 years in 2023, but more relevant to your retirement planning is the average life expectancy at age 65 — another 19.5 years, or 84.5.

You're probably a lot closer to age 65 than you are to age 0, so you ought to be using a life expectancy number that's much higher than you read in the newspaper. You ought to think closer to age 84 as your life expectancy, not age 78.

This one difference between the life expectancy of a 65-year-old as opposed to the life expectancy at birth explains almost all the difference in Americans' estimates of their personal longevity. According to the Center for Retirement Research at Boston College, the average 65-year-old male in America estimates his life expectancy at 77.4, and the average female estimates 78.2; meanwhile 83.2 and 85.7 are the true average life expectancies for 65-year-old males and females in America.[35]

LIFE EXPECTANCY AT AGE 65: ESTIMATED VS. ACTUAL

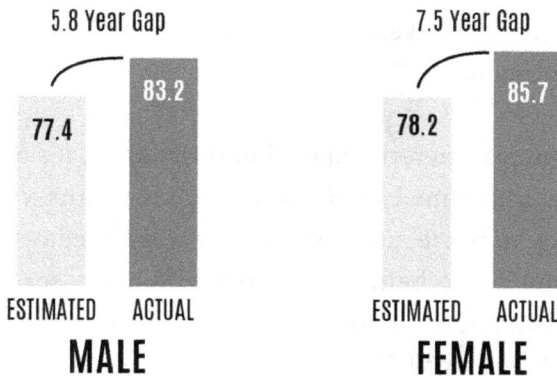

5.8 Year Gap   7.5 Year Gap

77.4 — 83.2   78.2 — 85.7

ESTIMATED ACTUAL   ESTIMATED ACTUAL

MALE   **FEMALE**

Since most people underestimate their life expectancy by six to seven years, the easy answer is just to add seven to the life expectancy number that popped into your head a few minutes ago. Of course, I prefer you to get a more personalized number, and I'll show you how to do that shortly, but I think you can appreciate now how misleading life expectancy news articles are when it comes to retirement planning.

YOUR RETIREMENT START AGE IS PROBABLY OFF TOO

The starting point of your retirement is another key component of your Retirement Longevity Number. And unfortunately,
many people get their retirement starting age wrong too.

The Employee Benefit Research Institute surveys workers
and retirees each year, and they consistently find two things
related to this topic.

1. The average worker expects to retire at age 65,
   but the average retiree actually retired at 62.
2. Roughly half of retirees retired earlier than
   they expected.[36]

Now, maybe this is good news, that the average retiree gets
three years more in retirement than they planned for, but in my
experience this three-year gap contributes to a lot of the anxiety
around retirement.

- If you plan to retire at 65, but retire at 62, it's often a sudden, unplanned retirement, which means you weren't
  ready to retire, and your money wasn't ready to retire!
- If you retire before age 65, you're often scrambling to
  find the best health insurance since you can't enroll in
  Medicare until 65.

And I think what's worst of all is how the combo of over-
estimating when you will retire and underestimating how long
you'll live affects your retirement math.

Imagine planning for retirement at 65 and living to 78. Your
money just needs to last thirteen years.

But the reality is more like retiring at 62 and living to 84.
Your money needs to last twenty-two years.

LENGTH OF RETIREMENT: ESTIMATED VS. ACTUAL

ACTUAL	22 years
ESTIMATED	13 years

AGE   62   64   66   68   70   72   74   76   78   80   82   84

I'm going to show you later on how twenty-two years might be too short of a time frame to plan for, but just going through those two numbers:

Retiring for twenty-two years, when you planned for thirteen years, means you need 70 percent more money just to get the same income over that longer lifetime.

Now, here's the easy fix for the starting part of the retirement longevity equation:

Get your money ready for retirement three years before you plan to retire.

That's great that you want to keep working until 65, but if you're not there yet, make sure your money is set up in the right mix of short-term and long-term investments three years ahead of time. You'll get

Get your money ready for retirement three years before you plan to retire.

three great benefits from being ready three years ahead of time.

1. You'll be ready in case you retire earlier than you expected.

This often happens when the market drops and companies lay off workers. If your investments are ready three years ahead of time, you'll likely be able to weather the down market that just cost you your job.

2. It's a lot easier walking into work knowing that you can walk out any time you want.

I've had several clients who have experienced this. They were planning to retire at 65, but they weren't excited to keep working.

I showed them they could retire today if they wanted to. We set up their investments and researched health insurance as if they would retire today, and then they kept on working because the stress was gone. They knew they were at work because they chose to be there, not because they had to be, and that made going into the office a whole lot more enjoyable.

3. Getting ready for retirement three years before you planned just might mean you can retire three years earlier than expected.

Remember Mike and Lisa from chapter 1? They didn't think they could retire for several years, but we went through the process. They created their Retirement Master Plan, and they pulled the trigger as soon as they were ready — years before they originally thought — and they haven't looked back!

HOW TO GET YOUR PERSONALIZED RETIREMENT LONGEVITY NUMBER

You've learned that your previous estimates for when you might retire and how long you might live need some updating. They are probably off by a combined nine years — and that's just talking through the averages.

When you're planning your own retirement, you need to rely on your own numbers, and thankfully they aren't too hard to find. Like I said earlier, it'll take you roughly five minutes total.

The first step is to think about when you want to retire. Perhaps it's age 62 or 65. Feel free to write down that age in your retirement plans, but when it comes to the spreadsheet you're working with, when it comes to what start age to plug into your retirement calculator, I suggest you plug in a number that's three years earlier than you originally planned for.

The second step is to create your personalized longevity estimate using an easy but accurate online calculator — my personal favorite to use is the Actuaries Longevity Illustrator (Longevityillustrator.org). I'll show you how next, but first, we need to talk about the third step.

The third step to creating your retirement longevity number is to understand that your retirement longevity number is probably wrong.

You might be thinking, "Why does Jeremy want me to estimate how long I'm going to live? Only God knows how long I'm going to live. What's the use in trying to figure out something you can't figure out? Didn't he just tell me earlier to focus on the things I can control?"

If you were thinking this, you are right. No one knows exactly how long they are going to live.

But everyone I talk to has a number in mind already, a number they've been using in their retirement plans.

I'm just asking you to use a more accurate number. And I'm asking you to think of what happens when you don't live to that exact age. Because you only have a 3.5 percent chance of dying exactly at your life expectancy age.[37] That means:

You have a 96.5 percent chance of dying either before or after your life expectancy age!

But that's not how people talk about it. I hear statements all the time like:

- "I'm going to live to 90."
- "I'll be lucky to make it into my 80s."
- "All the men in my family die at 70."

People talk about their life expectancy as if it's an exact number, but it's not — hardly anyone dies exactly at their life expectancy.

There's a reason why the actuaries use terms like "median" and "longevity" instead of "average" and "life expectancy."

You have a 96.5 percent chance of dying either before or after your life expectancy age!

They don't use "average," because they are trying to show the "median," the midpoint where half the people die before that age and half the people die after that age.

They don't use "life expectancy" because you shouldn't expect to live to a certain age — that will only happen 3.5 percent of the time.

Now, I'll admit that I often talk about "average life expectancy" in my *Mr. Retirement* YouTube videos because that's how normal people talk (sorry, actuaries). But in reality, I, and every other retirement expert out there, mean "median longevity."

And it's OK for you to keep saying "average life expectancy." But make sure you know that the true number to think about is "median longevity," which is the midpoint of how long people might live — half die before, and half die after that number.

You Need to Consider What Happens on Either Side of Your Personalized Longevity Estimate

When you get your personalized longevity estimate, you'll see that it's the age or length of time you're expected to live to 50 percent of the time. This number, this age, is not a certainty. It's a helpful tool, and I show you, in depth, how to use that tool at JeremyKeil.com.

So get your estimate, but when you have that number, I want you to take a few moments and consider how you, your spouse, and your family will be affected if you die before your longevity number and how you, your spouse, and your family will be affected if you live longer than your longevity number.

Every retirement decision you make should be based on what's most likely to happen, *and* it should be based on what happens if it doesn't work out the way you thought.

When you make your decisions around when to take your Social Security and pensions and how much you take out of your portfolio, consider what would happen if you live longer than average.

When you make decisions around life insurance, your pension survivorship option, whether to retire early, and whether to take that big trip this year, consider what would happen if you die sooner than average.

Now that you've learned how to get your personalized longevity estimate, how to use it to create your retirement longevity number, and how to think about that number as you make retirement decisions, it's time to go to an accurate, simple online calculator like the Actuaries Longevity Illustrator to get your own personalized longevity estimate.[38]

Go ahead, put down the book, discover your personalized longevity estimate, and when you're done — it should only take you five minutes — come back to chapter 12 to see how to master the biggest mindset shift in retirement: going from being a saver to being a spender.

CHAPTER 12

When The Paycheck Stops

Your heart may have just temporarily stopped when you read that chapter title.

When the paycheck stops.

It sounds so final. It sounds so scary. And you know what? That's OK.

It's OK to be afraid of taking money out of your retirement savings. You've never done it before!

You spent thirty-five years as a saver, and all of a sudden, in one day, you're supposed to become a spender?

Whether you've just retired, or you're just about to retire, you've probably spent some time wondering how you can possibly switch from being a saver to becoming a spender.

And you're not alone.

Roughly half of retirees are afraid to use their retirement savings.[39]

Retirees aren't just afraid of using their retirement savings; they are actually spending less than they could. Economists are generally baffled by this. Why would anyone who saves for retirement not use those retirement savings in retirement?

They have coined this phenomenon as the retirement consumption puzzle.[40]

Here's a quote from that economics paper: "Any rational agent will save before retirement, given that she expects a fall in income, and dissave after. However, we observe that individuals do the opposite: they dissave before and save after retirement."

Rational agent?

Dissave?

When you use terms like that, it seems to me that it's the economists who have it all wrong!

What I think they do have correct is that there is a fear of switching from a saver to a spender, a fear you have probably felt.

Some of that fear is completely rational. It makes sense to carry a little more in savings when you don't have a job. It makes sense to invest a little more conservatively when you're taking money out of your retirement savings.

But some of that fear drives actions that are irrational — actions that go against your retirement goals and dreams. My hope is that by the end of this chapter, you'll feel confident enough in your planning that you drive out the irrational part of this fear.

I think the big problem I see is that the current mindset is, "I'm a saver. How can I possibly become a spender?"

I believe that if you shift that mindset just a bit, you'll realize you're not changing who you are; you're just changing what you do.

You might view yourself as a *saver* right now, but I think you're really a *planner* who happens to save.

When you hit retirement, you're not turning into a *spender*. You didn't change who you are at all.

You're still a *planner*. It's just that now it's time in your plan to start spending.

You didn't change who you are.

You're just changing the tactic, to accomplish the strategy you've been planning for the past thirty-five years.

Let's see what happens when you don't make that mindset shift — when you're stuck in the thought that you can only be a saver or a spender, instead of living out who you really are: a planner.

WHEN YOU VIEW YOURSELF AS A SAVER, NOT A SPENDER

I had a meeting with my client, Jean, in August, and I asked how her summer was going.

"Oh, it's been awesome! I've spent a lot of time at the cabin, and most of the time, I've had my kids and grandkids visiting."

"That's so great," I replied. "I'm glad you've been enjoying your summer."

"Oh, for sure," Jean said. "The cabin is really my happy place."

And then Jean said something that took me completely by surprise.

"It's just too bad I have to sell it."

"Really? What's making you sell the cabin?" I asked her.

"Well, I'm getting older, and I really shouldn't be going on the roof anymore to clear the leaves from the gutters. And winter's coming next. It's such a long driveway, and it just takes me too long to clear the snow."

"That's too bad you have to sell it. I can tell how much you enjoy having your family there. Have you considered paying the neighbor kids to clear your gutters, or hiring a snow removal service?" I asked Jean.

"Oh, no, I couldn't possibly do that. That would cost too much! I'll just have to sell it. This will be the last summer at our family cabin." Jean said, looking a bit dejected.

I couldn't believe it, and I could not convince her otherwise. Jean was sitting on over $1 million in retirement accounts, and she wasn't taking one dollar out of them.

I figured that, at most, paying someone to clear her gutters and plow her driveway would cost her $1,000 per year — just a small fraction of the interest piling up in her accounts.

It was a shame. Jean's fear of spending even a small amount of the interest she was earning outweighed the idea of creating more memories at the cabin with her family.

This is the part of the retirement consumption puzzle that economists would call irrational behavior. Jean and her husband worked hard for their money; they saved for retirement, and if you had asked them years ago why they were saving, they probably would have said, "So I can enjoy my retirement," or "For my family."

But then, when it came to retirement time, time to use some of those hard-earned dollars to enjoy time with her family, Jean chose to hold on to the money instead of holding on to the family cabin.

Now, you might have guessed from the story that Jean is a widow. And I'd be willing to bet that experience has caused her to hold on to her money "just in case" — more than someone who is not widowed.

But I'm also willing to bet that a large reason she sold the family cabin is that she spent her whole life believing she was a saver, which is good, and that being a spender is bad. I believe that because Jean isn't alone.

I've worked with millionaire clients who have sold the house their kids grew up in instead of spending $20,000 on making their bathroom more wheelchair accessible. I've worked with grandmas who say, "I wish I could see my grandkids more, but the airplane tickets are too expensive these days," as they earn enough interest in their bank accounts each month to buy five airplane tickets.

WHEN YOU VIEW YOURSELF AS A PLANNER

There's another client I work with, Jane. She is also widowed, and that certainly colors how she views money. But Jane has been able to make the mindset shift that now that she's retired; she didn't switch from being a saver to being a spender.

Jane sees that she was a planner who saved when her husband was still living. She sees that he was a planner who bought life insurance "just in case."

And Jane sees that she's still a planner who is completing the plan that she and her husband put together years ago by changing the tactic and spending some of the money they've saved, as well as some of the money from the life insurance payout.

I believe that going through the Retirement Master Plan process helped Jane view herself as a planner who spends in a way that helps her and her family. But another part of our planning has helped, too — what I call permission money.

See, thanks to her Social Security and pension, Jane only "needs" $1,000 per month out of her investments to meet her monthly lifestyle amount and the rest of her retirement spending plan, but the saving and planning she and her husband did a long time ago and the projections she and I have done together, show that she can afford to take out $3,000 per month.

Now, she'd still like to hold on to some of that money; she'd still like to keep some money in reserve, and I think that's OK. She's holding some money in reserve to help her feel more confident in the amount she *is* spending.

Even though Jane only *needs* $1,000 per month from her investment accounts, she accepted my suggestion that she take out $2,500 from her investments.

In her retirement spending plan, we have that extra $1,500 per month listed as "permission money." She doesn't need that money, but she can afford to take it out, and if she didn't give herself permission to take it out on a monthly basis, I bet she never would.

Instead, the permission money comes out each month into her checking account and when the checking account gets higher than she really needs, she feels the permission to spend it.

For her, she spends it mostly on her family. She's planning a cruise with her kids and grandkids next year — and she's paying for the whole trip!

What a great use of her permission money. When she's nearing the end of her life, is she going to be comforted more by having an extra $20,000 in her investments or by knowing she did what she could to spend extra time with her family?

When she passes, and the kids inherit the remainder of her retirement accounts, are they going to talk with each other and say, "I'm sure glad this is $20,000 more than I thought it would be," or are they going to say, "I'm sure glad Mom took us on that trip!"

ADD PERMISSION MONEY TO YOUR RETIREMENT SPENDING PLAN

If you've read through this chapter and thought to yourself, "I'd rather be a Jane than a Jean," then head back to your retirement spending plan, look at your projections, and consider if you should add a new line item for permission money.

If your projections and your financial advisor's projections show that you can afford to take out more money than you need, think through how much of that extra you want to grant yourself permission to spend. I hope it's the vast majority of that extra amount.

You're not planning to spend that extra money because you're a "spender."

You're planning to spend that permission money because it's the natural next step in the retirement plans you've been making all along. Yes, the main tactic you used for years was "save," and the main tactic you will use for the rest of your life is "spend." But those are just tactics.

They are two parts of the same plan, and that's who you really are. You're not a "saver." You're not abandoning who you are to become a "spender." You're following who you have always been and who you always will be.

You're a planner.

Right now, you're planning, and when you hit retirement, be glad you've spent that time planning.

Because retiring is hard work!

CHAPTER 13

Retiring Is Hard Work

You'd be surprised how many people tell me, "Retiring is a lot of hard work!"

They had dreams of retiring today and hitting the beach tomorrow, but instead, there seems to be endless paperwork and countless decisions, each with a quick deadline, and not much help with how to make the best decision.

What's worse is that most of these decisions can't be changed. The most recent pension I helped someone take gave them eighteen days to change their mind. Social Security gives you twelve months to change your mind, but I've only met two people who have ever actually done that. And once you roll over your old 401(k) to an IRA, you can't put it back into the old 401(k)!

Those quick deadlines, and your inability to change your decisions are what make retirement so stressful. You want to get it right, but when you've never retired before, how do you know the steps to take and the mistakes to avoid?

The key to retiring today is putting in the time to learn your options and get it right. Thankfully, you're reading this book to make sure you're on the right track with your retirement. Unfortunately, most other Americans are not.

A few years back, Schwab did a survey that found that the average American spends four hours researching a car purchase, four hours researching their next vacation, and only two hours researching the investments in their 401(k).[41]

I give a lot of retirement planning webinars online. A lot of people show up to learn about retirement. Some of them ask us for more info on how we can help them plan their retirement; some of those folks become clients and we help them create their Retirement Master Plan.

I'm always trying to make sure we give the right info to the people on our webinars, so one day, I thought, "I wonder where these webinar attendees are in their retirement journey? How far in advance of retirement are they attending my educational webinar?"

Thankfully, I had the perfect dataset. Of the dozens of webinar attendees who started working with us as clients, I looked into exactly when they retired and when they had attended my webinar.

Half the people showed up to my webinar two years before they planned to retire. That's roughly what I expected would be the case for virtually everyone. I imagined that they wanted to retire, and they needed a plan to get ready to retire.

But then the other half surprised me. Half of my retirement planning webinar attendees were already retired. How can you plan for retirement when you're already retired?

Some people retired but then had all these questions about what to do and how to do it, and their advisor wasn't giving them the advice they wanted. It turns out some were let go, retirement was forced upon them, and they were quickly doing the work they needed to retire because they didn't have the chance to do it ahead of time.

What they had in common, though, was that they realized retiring was harder than they thought, and they needed a way to make it simpler.

YOU NEED TO MAKE A LOT OF DECISIONS AT RETIREMENT

When you hit retirement, you'll be faced with a lot of decisions you've never faced before.

Use the following as a starting point to create a checklist for your retirement, but make sure to add your own items, too, as you discover them.

1. Ask HR for a retirement packet from your company.
   - You're not asking to retire; you just want to see the info they give people at retirement so you can start planning out your decisions.
2. Ask HR how to file for your pension.
   - It doesn't start automatically when you retire, and you probably don't even start the pension through your company but instead through a third-party benefits manager.
3. Ask HR how you actually retire.
   - Is it a form you fill out? Does your manager have to approve? How much notice do you have to give?
4. Research your health insurance options and how you pay for them.
   - Don't assume that your retiree health insurance gets paid out of your pension.
5. Find out what happens to your remaining sick leave or PTO.
   - Will it get paid out, perhaps into an account? Or do you lose it?

6. Check into how your restricted stock or stock options vest when you retire.
   - You might want to retire after an award vests, not right before!
7. Check into how your bonus or long-term and short-term incentive plans will vest and pay out to you when you retire.
   - You might want to retire after your bonus or incentive money is in your pocket!
8. Look at how your deferred comp plans will pay out to you.
   - And now that you're retired, you may want to update your investment choices.
9. Decide if you'll convert your company life insurance, get your own, or maybe forego life insurance.
10. Make sure all your beneficiaries are correct on your 401(k), pension, life insurance, IRAs, and investment accounts.

Those are ten different things you'll either need to do now or should do right at retirement. There are probably several more you'll need to add to your list that are company-specific. Harley-Davidson, for example, gives eligible retirees a discount when buying a new motorcycle. That's worth checking into!

To download a PDF version of this retirement checklist so that you can use it in your retirement planning, visit JeremyKeil.com.

BEWARE OF DECISION FATIGUE

If looking at those ten areas started to cause you a lot of anxiety, you're not alone. Retiring *is* a lot of hard work but think of it as your final project — one where the payoff is a better retirement for you, not a better bottom line for your company.

I met John and Mary a few years back. John worked long hours in a physically demanding job. He wanted to retire ASAP, and I could see the weight of his job on his face and on Mary's face. I took them through the Retirement Master Plan process, and with each meeting and each decision, I could see the worries melt away.

We had figured out how best to take his pension, how he would get his health insurance, and even how to save some taxes on the employer stock within his 401(k). We set it up so that they would pay down $30,000 on their mortgage, pay off their car, and have enough money in the bank to live on for the rest of the year.

It seemed like he was all set, and John couldn't wait to check out of work. And check out of work he did. He retired in the summer and went about enjoying his newfound free time.

Until three months later, when Mary called me in a panic. Their health insurance was getting cancelled! It seems that in John's checkout state of mind, which frankly he had earned after putting in many years of hard work, he didn't bother opening his mail for the first three months of retirement.

Their health insurance wasn't being paid out of his pension, like John had assumed, but needed to be paid out of their bank account (as the several unread notices in the mail told him).

Thankfully, Mary opened his mail and called me just in time. We got it sorted out together, but the restful bliss of the beginning of their retirement quickly turned into the level of worry and anxiety that caused them to want to retire so badly in the first place!

You've worked hard in your career. After all your hard work, you deserve to enjoy your retirement. But don't let the stress of the act of retiring get in the way of your retirement happiness.

You've learned the five steps to create your Retirement Master Plan. Now, use those steps — along with the checklist in this chapter — to face the hard work of retiring and retire with confidence.

Before long, you'll be reaping the rewards of your hard work. But you might also face an unexpected challenge — one that you never saw coming. For years, you've wondered whether you'd have enough in retirement. But if you're like many retirees I meet, you may soon find out your biggest concern isn't running out of money — it's figuring out what to do with *too much!*

CHAPTER 14

You Might Spend Too Little

You've done the saving, you've done the planning, and you've finally retired, but now you're faced with a problem you probably didn't know you even had. It's a problem that economists call the "decumulation paradox."[42]

The decumulation paradox is that after years of working hard and saving what you can toward retirement, you finally reach retirement and then don't spend as much as you could.

You spend thirty-five years putting money into retirement so that you can take it out in retirement and then don't actually take the money out in retirement!

Now, the decumulation paradox is very similar to the retirement consumption puzzle in that retirees spend less than they could. The key distinction, I think, is that it's not just about economists being puzzled as to why retirees spend less than their financial models suggest. The paradox is that retirees say they want to spend their money and don't want to leave money behind, yet their actions show that they do the opposite.

Many retirees (48 percent) state that their number one goal is maintaining a comfortable standard of living, and only 3 percent say their number one goal is leaving an estate for their heirs.[43]

Yet, their actions, by not spending as much as they could from their investments, show that retirees often sacrifice their own spending and enjoyment in retirement (the highest goal for retirees) and leave more money for their heirs (a low-level goal).

RETIREMENT INVESTMENT: THEORY VS. REALITY

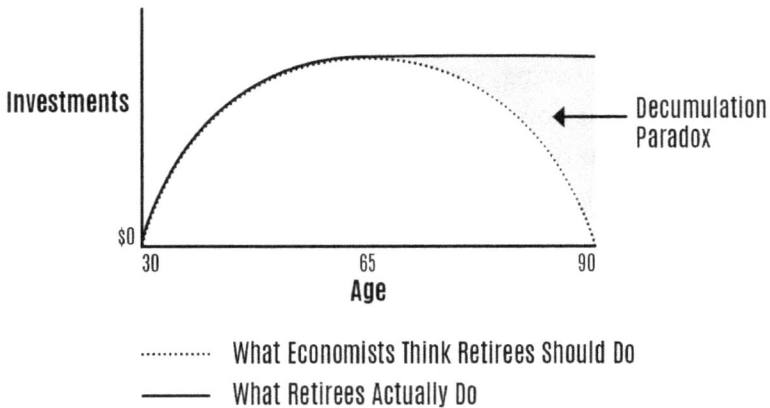

Investments

Decumulation Paradox

$0

30   65   90

Age

.... What Economists Think Retirees Should Do

——— What Retirees Actually Do

Why are retirees saying they want one thing yet doing another? Why is that a problem? And how might you set up your retirement portfolio to take advantage of this tendency?

I think there are three main reasons why retirees aren't spending as much as they should, and one big lesson on how to change your portfolio so you enjoy more of your hard-earned money during your well-deserved retirement.

WHY RETIREES AREN'T SPENDING AS MUCH AS THEY SHOULD

I've been observing retirees and how they spend money for over twenty years. Here's what I've learned:

1. Retirees hold on to their money "just in case."
2. Retirees feel better spending income than spending principal.
3. Retirees had a plan to put money into retirement but don't have a plan to take money out.

Now, these are my personal anecdotal summaries of retiree spending behavior, not scientific research, so I was excited when I came across research from the Society of Actuaries that found four key trends in how retirees spend their money.

1. Retirees prefer to spend their monthly income and try to avoid withdrawing from their investments.
2. Retirees prefer to hold on to their investments in case they are needed instead of taking regular income from their accounts.
3. Retirees take a wait-and-see approach to large expenses like home repairs and big medical bills, instead of planning ahead.
4. Retirees spend less throughout retirement, except on healthcare.[44]

I had some ideas ahead of time about why retirees do what they do, and reading this study showed I was on the right track.

I mentioned three reasons why retirees spend less than they should, but there's a fourth reason, really the one big reason that explains all the others — one that I believe many economists are not accounting for.

I often read studies that ask, "Why aren't retirees spending?" They suggest retirees are making "sub-optimal decisions," which is economist speak for "making bad choices."

I have a belief that all the differences between what retirees are doing and what economists think retirees should do come down to this one thing:

Retirees get comfort, even joy, when they add to their accounts and feel pain when they take money out.

Economists may be baffled at why retirees aren't spending as much as they could, but I think these four reasons explain why retirees don't spend as much as the financial models suggest.

1. Retirees hold on to their money "just in case."
2. Retirees feel better spending income than spending principal.
3. Retirees have a plan to put money into retirement but don't have a plan to take money out.
4. **Retirees get comfort, even joy, when they add to their accounts, and they feel pain when they take money out.**

You might not be retired yet, thinking, "That'll never happen to me," or you might already be retired, thinking, "Yep, that's me!"

However you're coming into this discussion, chances are your number one retirement priority is to "enjoy my retirement with the money I've saved," and a very low priority is to "leave an estate for my heirs." Yet many retirees spend their money as if these priorities were reversed.

When you learn why retirees feel this way and how you, too, are likely to feel this way, you can set up your retirement finances so that you actually make use of the money you've been saving in a way that matches your priorities.

Retirees Hold on to Their Money "Just in Case"

Retirees are smart. They know that their retirement might not go as planned, and just like when they were working, they spend less income than they make, holding on to the money "just in case."

Quite often, the two biggest just-in-case reasons to hold some money in reserve are outliving your money and long-term care expenses.

Will You Outlive Your Money?

Many retirees are worried about running out of money in retirement. That's why they are often researching the safe withdrawal rate — the percentage of money they can take out of their accounts without running out of money.

What's interesting about the safe withdrawal rate is that it's based on a worst-case scenario.[45] And thankfully, the worst-case scenario doesn't usually happen.

When you're focused on spending money based on the worst-case scenario, it's amazing what might happen even in an average scenario.

Michael Kitces did a study looking at the safe withdrawal rate research and asked, "What happens the rest of the time, when the worst-case doesn't happen?"

Michael's article, entitled "Why Most Retirees Will Never Draw Down Their Retirement Portfolio," has two very telling stats.

1. In two-thirds of the scenarios, retirees will more than double their investments from the beginning to the end of their retirement.
2. Retirees are more likely to 5x their wealth than to finish with less money than they started with.[46]

For retirees, focusing on not running out is wise, but thankfully, less likely to happen than perhaps they thought.

Will You Need Long-Term Care?

Now, you read earlier my bias toward long-term care insurance and why I feel that way. But as you've talked to your friends about whether they have long-term care insurance, you've realized that most people don't.

It seems the number one way retirees prepare for the risk of future long-term care costs is by spending less money overall, just in case they need the money for long-term care.

If retirees are holding on to their money just in case they need it for long-term care costs, the big question is, "Will they really need to pay for their long-term care?"

The answer is, "Maybe, maybe not."

You might have heard this stat from an often-quoted study. I've certainly heard it plenty of times:

"70 percent of Americans will need long-term care."[47]

Often, that stat is quoted by the person trying to sell you long-term care insurance!

What's not brought up is another stat, perhaps a little more telling:

48 percent of Americans 65-plus will receive *paid* long-term care services over their lifetime.[48]

So, chances are, ever so slightly, that you won't need to pay for long-term care services at all in your retirement.

Here's another stat from the same study:

Only 24 percent of older adults receive more than two years of paid long-term care services.[49]

Now, part of me sees that 70 percent of Americans need long-term care services, but only 48 percent of them receive them, and I think, "Aha, if they had the insurance, they'd probably get the care they need."

But I think a bigger part of the story is that you're probably saving up for long-term care costs that are only significant 24 percent of the time.

Just like in the "What if I run out of money?" scenario, the "What if I need to pay a lot of money for my long-term care costs?" question is leading retirees to hold on to their money for scenarios that aren't likely to happen.

Retirees Feel Better Spending Income than Spending Principal

Take a minute to go through these two thought experiments:

Imagine you go to work for just one hour, and when you leave, your boss pays you $20 in cash.

Now, imagine you volunteer for one hour, and when you go back to your car, you find a $20 bill in the parking lot.

Which $20 bill are you more likely to spend? The $20 you earned or the $20 you found?

I'm willing to bet you're more likely to spend the found money. Now, imagine you have $1,000 in the bank and you earn $20 interest. Now you have $1,020.

Imagine, instead, you bought a stock for $1,000, and it grew to $1,020 in value.

You have the same amount of money. You have the same amount of gain.

But which account are you more likely to take the $20 from? The $20 in interest from your savings account, or would you sell the $20 in gains in your brokerage account?

Financially and economically speaking, it doesn't really matter, yet again I'm willing to bet you are far more likely to spend the $20 of interest you earned in your savings account than you are to sell enough shares of stock to take out the $20 in gains from your brokerage account.

Whether it's wanting to hold on to money you earned but spending money you found, or it's wanting to hold on to the growth in value but spending the same growth through interest, human beings, whether retired or not, exhibit this same pattern time and time again.

You care far more about something you already have than something that just showed up.

When interest or dividends or your pension or Social Security hit your bank account, you feel confident in spending that money — partly because you expect to get more of that same money next month, but also because it just showed up. You haven't held on to that money long enough to feel like it's yours. You haven't felt the ownership of that new money long enough to think, "I've got to hold on to this."

I see it happen all the time with my clients, especially when it comes to the interest and dividends within taxable brokerage accounts. At the end of the year, I might review their accounts and say, "You earned $12,000 in interest and dividends this year. What would you like to do with it?"

They'll tell me back, "Oh, just let it stay in there. I don't need it."

They've already felt ownership; they don't want to lose what they already have.

But then, five minutes later, if I ask them, "For next year, I project $12,000 in interest and dividends — $1,000 per month. Would you like me to have your brokerage account send that money to your checking account each month?"

They'll tell me back, "Oh, that's a great idea. I've got a few projects I want to do, and I could use the money."

They haven't felt the ownership yet — those dividends and interest don't feel like money they have, but money that just showed up — and they can't wait to spend the income.

You've probably seen yourself in these situations. You've probably said something like, "I want to hold on to my principal and spend the interest."

It doesn't seem that the retirement researchers get this the way retirees do. Maybe it's because they haven't retired yet!

Part of me understands what the researchers are thinking. After all, you started your retirement savings journey with zero, and you built up a good amount of wealth with the whole point of spending that money you saved.

But the other part of me realizes that once you've built up that money, you want to hold onto it. It's just human nature. And I think a lot more of the retirement research needs to understand it's OK for humans to act like humans!

Retirees Had a Plan to Put Money Into Retirement But Don't Have a Plan to Take Money Out

If you ask the average 50-year-old to define "retirement planning," I bet their definition would really boil down to "saving for retirement." It wouldn't include figuring out how much they can live on in retirement, when to take Social Security, how to save on taxes, or which accounts to take money from in retirement.

It seems like a lot of investors and the investing community are focused on getting to retirement. They're focused on investing, or like the old ING commercials said, hitting their "retirement number."[50]

With all this focus on and planning for hitting retirement, it seems that most retirees don't plan for how to take money out in retirement.

The Teachers Insurance and Annuity Association (TIAA) Institute conducted a survey that found the average retiree doesn't take any money out of their retirement accounts until at least four years after retirement. They found that 52 percent of retirees didn't take out any money at all from their retirement accounts until they were forced to do so by required minimum distributions (RMDs).

TIAA's conclusion is that "an RMD is becoming the de facto default distribution choice for retirees."[51]

My conclusion is that when retirees aren't taught how to turn their retirement savings into retirement income, *their* plan defaults to the *government's* plan.

And I think, too, that if you don't have a specific plan to take money out of your accounts, the safest thing to do is to not take money out at all. That seems to be what most retirees are doing. A study by New York Life found that only 16 percent of retirees were taking money out of their accounts on a systematic basis.[52]

With all the effort and sacrifice that goes into saving for retirement and so few retirees intentionally taking money out of retirement accounts, perhaps we're beginning to see the paradox that leaves so many retirement researchers puzzled: Why bother saving for the future if you don't actually use the money?

Retirees Get Comfort, Even Joy, When They Add to Their Accounts and Feel Pain When They Take Money Out

If you've ever saved for retirement, you've experienced the joy of adding money to your accounts. You get your statement every quarter, and it feels good when it goes up. It feels good to know that you're saving money for the future. It's comforting to know that you're setting aside money so you'll be OK if things go bad.

And those same feelings don't go away in retirement; in fact, they are magnified because now you're expected to take money out of your accounts instead of putting money in.

Your feelings of safety and comfort begin to be stripped away as you see negatives on your statement each month as you take money out of your account.

Remember Mike and Lisa from chapter 1? I think they've got their Retirement Master Plan pretty well put together. They're making good use of their retirement savings and retirement income, *and* every month, they put $100 back into their investment account.

They like the idea of saving for the future, saving for the "just in case," and while it seems completely illogical to take $3,100 per month out of one's accounts *and* send $100 per month right back into their accounts, I think it's somewhat genius.

Humans like to save for the future. Humans like to see a positive on their account statements. Good retirement savers got to where they are because they saved every month into their retirement accounts.

If you need to take out just a little less than you can afford in order to feel comfortable in retirement, I think that's OK. If you need to keep putting money aside each month toward your savings, that's also OK.

What's not OK, though, is letting all these natural human tendencies we just discussed prevent you from enjoying the benefits of the savings you worked so hard to build.

HOW TO GET MORE ENJOYMENT FROM YOUR RETIREMENT SAVINGS

You've learned that economists believe there is a decumulation paradox in that people spend their working careers saving for their retirement future, and when their retirement future comes, they don't take out nearly as much income as they could, despite saying that's what they want to do.

You've learned the four reasons retirees aren't spending as much as they could, which means they're ignoring their number one goal of supporting their own standard of living and, instead, are leaving more money to their kids — a low-priority goal.

The question now is, "How will you adjust your Retirement Master Plan so you can both have more fun *and* satisfy the psychological needs to hold on to your money in retirement?"

Here are some ideas on how to approach your retirement planning decisions so that they can bring you more enjoyment and less worry throughout your retirement.

A Better Way To Take Care of Your "Just in Case"

Retirees are often holding onto their money just in case. Let's dig into the "just in case" and whether holding onto one's money is the best way to accomplish that.

The Society of Actuaries has been conducting a retirement risk survey every two years since 2001.[53] Consistently, the top concerns of retirees revolve around running out of money and the cost of long-term care services.

If your top concerns are similar, then I would encourage you to consider:

- Finding ways to get more guaranteed lifetime income.
- Creating a long-term care plan and perhaps buying insurance for it.

If you're concerned about running out of money, then tilting your retirement investments toward accounts that will *never* run out of money is a great way to match the investments you use to the risks you are concerned about.

Delaying Social Security, taking a monthly pension instead of a lump-sum payout, or even buying a lifetime income annuity are all ways designed to make your money last your whole lifetime.

When it comes to "What if I need the money for long-term care costs," making sure you have a long-term care plan should help you there, too.

Instead of holding back on taking money from all of your accounts, perhaps just set aside a long-term care fund and choose to not take money from that particular account, so the money is there for the just in case of long-term care costs.

You should feel more free to spend out of your other accounts, knowing that your long-term care costs are planned for in your long-term care fund.

Or perhaps take a second look at long-term care insurance. If you know that an insurance company is planning to help you pay for the cost of your long-term care, then you should feel more confident in spending your money. You don't have to hold back money from your monthly income when someone else is committed to helping you pay that potential cost.

This isn't just theory — the Employee Benefit Research Institute found that retirees who bought long-term care insurance spent about 10 percent more in retirement than those without.[54] This 10 percent extra spending was after controlling for income and wealth, so the extra spending wasn't caused by having more income or money.

It seems that retirees who have long-term care insurance feel free to spend that 10 percent more instead of holding onto it in reserve because they feel confident that their insurance is the reserve they need for future long-term care costs.

Enjoy Your Principal More by Turning It Into Income

You learned earlier that people would rather spend income than dip into their principal. They'd rather use interest and dividends than sell part of their investments. They'd rather receive an automatic payout instead of having to withdraw from their accounts.

If the goal of your retirement investments is to generate income, but you're hesitant to spend down your assets, the key is to turn some of your investment accounts into income accounts. That way, you'll actually use and enjoy the income they produce!

One of the most effective ways to create more retirement income is by delaying Social Security. This strategy sets you up for a higher income in the future, but it comes with a challenge.

Delaying benefits means you'll need to withdraw money from your own accounts to replace the income you would have received had you claimed Social Security earlier. And as we've seen, spending down investments — even as part of a solid plan — can feel surprisingly difficult!

One solution I've found is to create a Social Security Bridge. Instead of taking income from Social Security today, you could set aside a chunk of your money and start withdrawing the same amount you would have received from Social Security to live on as income.

The payment into your checking account is no different than if you had started Social Security. Your spending doesn't have to change. You've just chosen to live off a part of your investments for a little while as your Social Security grows, and then when your Social Security starts, it replaces the amount you were getting from your Social Security Bridge.

You could set it up as a bond ladder or CD ladder, where money comes due periodically — just in time to pay it out to you.

You could also find an account through an insurance company called a period certain annuity, where the insurance company pays out the money to you each month. It might pay out less interest than setting up the bond or CD ladder on your own, but it's less work for you, and it's guaranteed by the insurance company.

This period certain annuity is the solution I used for my client Kevin. I told him that we could set up a CD ladder, with CDs coming due each quarter, and when they came due, we would transfer the funds into his checking account to live on. He wasn't too enthusiastic about it, saying, "This seems like a lot of work just to use my own money!"

I described to him how the period certain annuity worked, in that he handed over a chunk of money to the insurance company, and they started paying him money each month into his bank account. The insurance company figured out a guaranteed interest rate that didn't change, and they figured out the monthly payments so that all of his principal and interest were paid back to him over five years.

Kevin, who had worked in banking his whole life, thought about it for a moment and then said, "It's like a reverse mortgage for my money. I love it!" And love it he did. Each month for five years, he got a payment into his checking account that he felt comfortable spending while he waited on Social Security.

Kevin felt more comfortable delaying Social Security because he knew he had a guaranteed payment coming into his checking account each month. He felt more comfortable spending the money he got each month from his Social Security Bridge, partly because we set it up in a way that was easy for him. But also, I think he got more enjoyment from that monthly payment because it felt more like an income and less like he was cashing in part of his investments.

By creating a Social Security Bridge and setting up his payments more like income than a withdrawal, Kevin got the benefit of both higher Social Security in the future and added enjoyment from his investments today.

Whether it's choosing a Social Security Bridge like Kevin, a monthly pension instead of the lump-sum option, or perhaps even a monthly guaranteed lifetime income from an annuity, shifting investment dollars toward income dollars sure seems to help you worry less and be happier in retirement.

Plan Your Retirement Withdrawals

A few years ago, my client Steve retired. When we started discussing how much to withdraw from his accounts each month, he confidently said, "I don't need money each month. My pension and Social Security are enough."

But based on his retirement spending plan, I knew otherwise. His guaranteed income wasn't quite enough to cover his lifestyle spending amount, and after thirty-five years of saving, he had $500,000 set aside for retirement — money he had worked hard for and deserved to enjoy.

Steve retired, and then, about a month later, he called me, right around the 25th of the month, and said, "Can you send me $500? My car needs new tires. I just need a little extra — this will be the last time."

Then, toward the end of the next month, Steve called me up and said, "Can you send me $1,000? My wife had a minor surgery, but she's all good now, and this will be the last time."

Then, toward the end of the next month, he called me up again and said, "Can you send me $1,500? My kid needs a little extra to help pay for my grandson's tuition that's due."

This kept on happening every one to three months. Every time, I would say, "Steve, why don't we just start sending you money every month," and he would say, "I don't need money each month. It's just this one-time thing, and this will be the last time."

Every time he called, I could hear the stress in his voice, and I can't imagine the amount of stress he was going through each month, toward the end of the month, as his checking account was running toward $0 and he was deciding whether he could make it to the first or if he needed to call and ask for money out of his accounts again.

After a couple of years, I finally convinced Steve to start taking $1,000 out of his accounts each month.

And then he stopped calling.

It's kind of sad, in a way. I like Steve. I like talking to him. But, I still get to see him four times a year during our quarterly planning meetings. And instead of calling me nearly every month with worry in his voice, every time I see him, he's got a big smile on his face!

HAVE FUN, PURPOSE, AND HAPPINESS IN YOUR RETIREMENT

You've worked hard to save toward your retirement all these years. Sometimes it seems that retiring itself is hard work. But it's worth it.

Retirement is a time to enjoy the fruits of your labor. Retirement is a time to pause and then reinvent yourself.

It doesn't cost money to have fun, purpose, and happiness in retirement, but sometimes a little extra money can help you pursue your fun, purpose, and happiness.

As you go about creating your Retirement Master Plan, remember the goal is not to get every decision right. The goal is not to create a beautiful plan, but a beautiful life.

Money is a tool; it's not the goal. As you create your Retirement Master Plan, focus on the fun, the purpose, the happiness your money can help create for yourself and your family.

You've learned the steps you need to create your Retirement Master Plan. You've learned the fears that can get in the way.

You've learned what to do and what not to do. And now it's time to create your dream retirement.

CHAPTER 15

Create Your Dream Retirement

Retirement used to be a far-off point in your future, but at some point, it starts to become real.

Maybe your kids graduated from college, and you finally have time to think about what's next for you.

Maybe you have reached one of the "planning ages," like 55, 59½, 62, or 65, and you realize that retirement could become a specific date, not a generic concept.

Maybe your company just let you go, and you're wondering if you're retired or just unemployed.

No matter what caused you to pick up this book and start planning for your retirement today, there's a reason you did: you want to create your dream retirement.

You might be waiting to realize that dream because you think you haven't saved enough for retirement or done enough to be ready for retirement. Most retirees I talk to would say to take the plunge, whether you feel ready or not.

I would tell you two things:

1. Retiring brings you the biggest financial decisions of your life.

When to retire, where to live, when to take Social Security, and which Medicare option to choose are just some of the decisions.

Don't retire until you've thought it through, answered those questions, and sidestepped the big $100,000 mistakes that many retirees make.

2. Retirement is not about letting go of who you were; it's about taking control of who you are.

Retirement isn't the piece of paper that tells your job you're quitting; retirement is the act of taking control of your life.

If you want to retire today, retire today. If you want to change jobs or go part-time, then change jobs or go part-time.

I didn't name this book *Retire Today* because today is the day you should quit your job, although maybe you'll feel confident enough to do that!

I named this book *Retire Today* because I believe today is the day you can learn how to retire; today is the day you can take the steps to improve your retirement; today is the day you can take control and make the retirement decisions you need to make so that you can live your dream retirement.

Lori called my office a few years back because she was facing one of those retirement planning ages, 62, and she had just moved into a management job and wasn't enjoying it.

To say she was a little stressed out about finances would be an understatement. She found my info online and called in because her previous financial advisor left his company, and her account was transferred to a new advisor.

When I walked into my conference room, Lori was sitting there with her arms crossed. She laid it all on the table — not just her account statements, but exactly how she felt:

"I'm almost 62. I'm trying to figure out if I can retire, and I have no idea what I'm doing with my investments. I don't want to see a repeat of 2008 and watch my investments drop in half just before I retire.

"The health system I work for just moved me to a management job that I didn't want to take, but I felt like I had to, just so I could have enough money to retire. Then, my investment company handed my accounts to the new guy. I've never met this person, and I'm supposed to have them plan my retirement?

"They're a brand-new financial advisor — they can't know that much about retirement planning. I've been burned by a financial advisor before, so I need someone I can trust, someone who can teach me about my money, and someone who can help me feel confident that I can retire in five years at 66½. Can you do that for me?"

As you can imagine, my next words would determine whether we'd be working together or she'd be walking out.

"You've got a lot of big decisions ahead of you, and you haven't been getting the help you wanted. Can I walk through the process we use, and then you can decide if it's the right way for you to approach things?"

"Let's hear it," said Lori, so I got up from my chair, walked over to the whiteboard, and began to draw out and describe how she could create her Retirement Master Plan using the five simple steps you've learned in this book.

I saw her face soften as she unfolded her arms, leaned in, and started to ask questions and give me info on when she wanted to retire, her pension and Social Security, her 401(k), and how she wanted to pay off her mortgage before she retired.

"How does this process sound?" I asked Lori.

"It's exactly what I'm looking for," said Lori, "but can I retire?"

"I'm sure you *can* retire," I told her, "But the question is *when* can you retire and with *how much* income. I don't know that today, but if you'd like, we can figure that out together."

"Yes, I'd like that. How can we get started?" asked Lori.

"Well, I see you brought your computer. If we can pull up some of your financial info, then we can get started today. We'll need to get:

- Your Social Security statement.
- Your latest tax return.
- Your 401(k) statement and something called your Summary Plan Description that describes all the rules for your 401(k).
- Your pension info and the Summary Plan Description for that pension.
- Information on your retiree health plan, if you have one."

"That's why I brought my computer. I need to figure out if I can retire. Let's get started," said Lori.

We pulled up her computer, and I started digging into the info we needed. Then, I had to give her some unfortunate news when it came to her pension.

"You said earlier, Lori, that your pension retirement age is 66½. I see on your projection page that the retirement age is actually 67, and I confirmed that when I looked at your plan documents. It's not a horrible difference, but it is a difference, and I want to make sure you know the true number."

"That's disappointing. That's why I want to retire at 66½," said Lori. "That's not what I wanted to hear today, but I guess I'm better off knowing that now. My whole plan was to work until 66½ and then retire when I got my full pension. I guess now I have to work until 67. At least I know this ahead of time and won't get blindsided when I try to retire at the wrong time."

"Yes, it is better to know ahead of time," I told her. "But we'll see if that pension difference even matters. I've got everything I need to get started. Let me take a look at all this, put some ideas together, and let's get back together in two weeks."

When we got back together, I shared my ideas with Lori, based on when she wanted to retire and how much risk she was willing to take to get there.

"Lori, you've saved well, and I think you're in a better spot than you thought previously. Here's what I recommend:

- You only have $50,000 left on your mortgage. You wanted to pay that off before you retire, but you have enough in your savings and your Roth IRA to pay that off right now. If you pay that off now, that could take away the financial pressure you feel that pushed you toward that management job you don't want.
- You're quite nervous about the stock market, and you don't want to 'repeat 2008 again,' especially when you're less than five years away from retiring. Your investments are currently 75 percent in the stock market.
  - I suggest moving one-third of your investments to a money market so that you have money set aside and don't have to rely on the stock market for the first few years of your retirement.
  - The other two-thirds of your investments should be moved to a moderate investment, with 60 percent in the stock market.

- o Overall, your stock market percentage would be cut to 40 percent stocks from the current 75 percent.
- You planned on working full-time and then retiring at 66½. I think that you've saved well enough, and you have your pension and Social Security, so that you could completely retire at age 65. The big thing for you is getting health insurance and getting the most from your pension and Social Security.
  - o If you wait on your pension and Social Security just a little bit longer than you had previously thought, that will help you get more retirement income in the long run.
  - o And if you move money out of the stock market into the money market, that will make sure you have money set aside for the first few years of your retirement so that you can retire when you want to and not have to worry about a repeat of 2008 again.

"When you do all that, I believe you'll be able to retire at 65 and have the income you'd like — you wouldn't need to work until 67 or even 66½ like you thought. And I know your management job pays you $20,000 more than before, but I don't think you need that extra money to make this work. If you can, I suggest you go back to your old job so you don't have as much stress."

"Wow, I thought I'd have to stick it out in a job I hate for four more years!" said Lori. "I'm glad to hear, too, that the difference in the pension won't ruin my retirement. And I like the idea of paying off my house and getting more conservative with my investments."

Lori followed her Retirement Master Plan and moved her investment risk down, not because I wanted her to time the market or that I was predicting a market drop, but because her investments were not previously set up based on her risk level or when she needed to start taking money out.

She didn't yet feel comfortable switching out of the higher pay (and higher stress) of her manager role, but then COVID-19 hit, and the stress level of any healthcare position went through the roof.

During our (Zoom) meeting in April 2020, Lori asked me, "Do I need to get more conservative with my investments? I don't want to lose any more."

I reminded her, "We already moved one-third of your 401(k) over to the money market — that money hasn't dropped at all. And we don't want to make a quick, short-term decision on your long-term money. You're not planning on using that money for several years. Let's keep it invested for the long-term because that's when you need it: in the long term."

After seeing the market recover in the fall of 2020 and seeing her Retirement Master Plan work out for over a year, Lori finally felt comfortable quitting her management role and moving back into her previous role, working directly with patients.

She loved that role so much that, despite my telling her she didn't need to work at the age of 65, she kept on working for two more years on a part-time basis. Soon after she went part-time at 65, I asked Lori how she was doing, and she said, "I'm in heaven. I'm living the dream!"

After dropping to two days a week and then moving to one day a week, she eventually got to where she had too much she wanted to do outside of work, and she fully retired. She wanted to celebrate by taking my wife and me out to dinner — and insisted on paying!

I asked Lori what she planned to do with her free time, and she said, "I've always wanted to learn how to ride a motorcycle. I'm signed up to start classes next week!"

Lori has a lot less stress and is a lot happier every time I see her. She walked into my office feeling like she had to take a job she didn't want and wondering how she could possibly retire five years later.

She kept taking steps, making the decisions that would help create the stability she was looking for in her retirement.

Even though she didn't retire the day she walked into my office, she started taking control of her retirement the day she walked into my office.

And that's the goal of your Retirement Master Plan. That you take control, so you can rely on the math instead of the guesswork.

I believe that when you take that control, you give yourself the best opportunity to make more retirement income, pay less in retirement taxes, and avoid big retirement mistakes.

It's time for you to start putting the puzzle pieces of your retirement together. It's time to create your own Retirement Master Plan.

Next, I'm going to show you where to start. Who knows, maybe you'll be like Lori, who finally said goodbye to the job she didn't like and, quite literally, rode off into the sunset!

CHAPTER 16

Put Your Puzzle Pieces Together

You've read all the books, you've watched all the videos, you've talked it over with your spouse; you're ready to retire today.

But where do you start?

How do you begin to put the different pieces of your retirement puzzle together? How do you create your Retirement Master Plan?

Start with the acronym PIE (plan, implement, enjoy):

Plan your retirement.
Implement your plan.
Enjoy your life.

When I talk to someone who is contemplating retirement, they often don't know where to begin. They don't know how to plan their retirement, and their current financial advisor hasn't been teaching them how to do it.

They're afraid to begin their retirement because they're afraid to make a mistake. They don't know where to start or who to turn to. What they need is a plan to help them look at their retirement from all angles so they can avoid big retirement mistakes.

Other people I talk to have their plan, but they haven't pulled the trigger on retirement. They have a lot of spreadsheets, they've created a lot of scenarios, but they still haven't retired. What's holding them back is the fear of missing something.

They know they've planned it out, but what if their plans are missing an important factor they haven't considered? They often tell me, "I don't know what I don't know." They don't know who they can trust to consider all the angles, double-check their work, and improve their plans where they can be improved.

And some people have yet to retire because they forgot the true goal of retirement planning. The true goal is not to optimize your tax situation; it's not to keep growing your money, although both of those things are helpful.

The true goal of saving for retirement is to enjoy your retirement. Don't arrange your life to make your spreadsheet happy. Arrange your money to make your life happy.

Whether you're afraid of making a big mistake, afraid of missing something in your planning, or you're focusing more on your retirement spreadsheet than your retirement happiness, follow PIE to create your successful retirement.

PLAN

There's an interesting paradox when it comes to retirement.

The money you have won't make you happy, but your money worries can make you unhappy.

As much as your retirement success will come from all your non-financial decisions, making sure you've taken care of your finances will allow you the confidence to focus on those more important non-financial decisions.

You're holding the key to your retirement plans right now. I've laid out, in chapters 6–10, exactly how to create your Retirement Master Plan in five simple steps. These chapters will show you how to figure out your:

- Retirement spending plan
- Lifetime income plan
- Tax-smart retirement plan
- Retirement investment plan
- Legacy protection plan

But don't jump back to chapter 6 right away. Go first to chapter 11 to discover your retirement longevity number.

In the math of retirement planning, your retirement longevity number is the most important factor.

Before you create a budget, before you invest your money, spend some time learning how to project out how long you'll live in retirement and how to protect yourself and the people you care about from the very real, close to 100 percent probability that you will live longer, or shorter, than your planned number.

If you've listened to my podcasts or seen my YouTube videos, you've probably heard me talk about the math of retirement. The math of retirement is very powerful — it can help you if you use the math, and it can harm you if you ignore the math.

I encourage you to learn the math, do the math, and follow the math of retirement. Learning the math and doing the math are a part of your planning. Following the math is when you've realized that your plans are solid and that it's time to implement your planning.

IMPLEMENT

While the math of retirement will help you in your planning and decision-making, remember that the retirement math is not your only consideration, and that the math of retirement can change.

Some people make poor retirement decisions because they ignore the math, and others make poor choices because they are creating a math-focused retirement plan.

I met Mark this past year after he attended one of my retirement planning webinars. Mark's a smart guy, and he's done well with investing, but he's having a little trouble creating his retirement plan — and I think that's the trouble; he's focused on a plan and not the planning.

He just wrote me, "I'm trying to find a formula that would guide me on how to complete Roth conversions over the next thirty years to minimize lifetime taxes for me, my wife, and my kids. I also need a detailed, numbers-driven analysis of the best strategy for my IRA withdrawals and Roth conversions in the years ahead. And I need to know in the greatest detail possible the appropriate asset allocation for my traditional and Roth IRAs."

I'm glad Mark is trying to figure out what's best for him and his wife (and his kids). That's a worthy goal.

What I'm working on with him right now is something I often work on with smart, analytical retirees: understanding that *the planning* is more important than *the plan*. Running the retirement math won't give you the one perfect solution that makes everything work, but it will help you discover the right direction for your decisions.

I do want you to *learn* the math, I want you to *do* the math, and I want you to *follow* the math, but at the same time, heed the words of Moshe Milevsky, one of the greatest minds in creating and studying retirement math.

"Math will never solve retirement planning."[55]

This is coming from the author of *The Calculus of Retirement Income* and *The 7 Most Important Equations for Your Retirement.*

The math is important. The math will help you calculate your retirement income needs and how to get there. The math will help you implement your decisions — just remember these wise words from Moshe Milevsky:

"There's much more to a satisfying, healthy and fulfilling retirement than 'solving it.'"[56]

ENJOY

As you plan your retirement, as you fill out your pension, Social Security, and tax forms, keep in mind the goal isn't a perfect spreadsheet, it's not optimizing and maximizing every part of your finances.

The goal is a satisfying, healthy, and fulfilling retirement.

Do the planning.

Learn the math, do the math, and follow the math.

Implement those decisions.

But do all of that knowing that the goal of creating your Retirement Master Plan is not *creating* a Retirement Master Plan.

The goal of creating your Retirement Master Plan is to enjoy your life.

You're trying to make more income, pay less in taxes, and avoid big retirement mistakes so that you can have more freedom and more time to enjoy your life.

The key to retirement planning isn't even to *retire*. It's to enjoy your life, starting right now.

If you've done your retirement planning and you choose to keep working because you enjoy working, then you have succeeded.

203

If you've done the math and you decide to do something that makes you happy, even though it doesn't make your spreadsheet happy, then you have succeeded.

And if you've discovered your retirement longevity number, gone through all five steps, and created your Retirement Master Plan, then it's time to move beyond the money and give yourself the permission to retire today.

Endnotes

1   Jasmine Escalera, "Retirement Fears," LiveCareer, https://www.livecareer.com/resources/retirement-fears.

2   Fritz Gilbert, "Introducing the 90-10 Rule of Retirement," *The Retirement Manifesto*, https://www.theretirementmanifesto.com/introducing-the-90-10-rule-of-retirement/.

3   "Fixed Income Annuity Calculator," Charles Schwab, https://www.schwab.com/annuities/fixed-income-annuity-calculator.

4   David Altig, Laurence J. Kotlikoff, and Victor Yifan Ye, "How Much Lifetime Social Security Benefits Are Americans Leaving on the Table?" Working Paper 30675 (National Bureau of Economic Research, November 2022), https://www.nber.org/system/files/working_papers/w30675/w30675.pdf.

5   *Breakeven Returns for Delayed Social Security Claiming* (PGIM DC Solutions, 2024), https://www.pgim.com/us/en/institutional/insights/asset-class/multi-asset/dc-solutions/breakeven-returns-for-delayed-social-security-claiming.

6   "Longevity Illustrator," Society of Actuaries and American Academy of Actuaries, https://www.longevityillustrator.org/.

7   "Fixed Income Annuity Calculator," https://www.schwab.com/annuities/fixed-income-annuity-calculator.

8   "Guaranteed Income Estimator," Fidelity, https://digital.fidelity.com/prgw/digital/gie/.

9   "Income Annuity Quote Calculator," ImmediateAnnuities.com, https://www.immediateannuities.com/.

10 Dave Ramsey, "Should I Take My Pension in Payments or as Lump Sum?" *The Ramsey Show Highlights*, YouTube, September 21, 2019, 4:41, https://www.youtube.com/watch?v=mVyt_GdgKOk.

11 *2025 Social Security Changes* (Social Security Administration, fact sheet, 2025), https://www.ssa.gov/news/press/factsheets/colafacts2025.pdf.

12 David McKnight, *The Power of Zero, Revised and Updated: How to Get to the 0% Tax Bracket and Transform Your Retirement* (Crown, 2018).

13 "Capital Gains and Losses," Tax Topic 409 (Internal Revenue Service), https://www.irs.gov/taxtopics/tc409.

14 "Federal Income Tax Rates and Brackets" (Internal Revenue Service), https://www.irs.gov/filing/federal-income-tax-rates-and-brackets.

15 "Core S&P 500 ETF," iShares, https://www.ishares.com/
us/products/239726/ishares-core-sp-500-etf; "Core US
Aggregate Bond ETF," iShares, https://www.ishares.com/
us/products/239458/ishares-core-total-us-bond-market-etf.

16 Ryan Ermey, "Stocks and Bonds Both Down: What to
Do with Your Money," *CNBC Make It*, October 18, 2022,
https://www.cnbc.com/2022/10/18/stocks-and-bonds-both-
down-what-to-do-with-your-money.html.

17 "Time, Not Timing, Is What Matters in Investing," Capital
Group, https://www.capitalgroup.com/individual/planning/
investing-fundamentals/time-not-timing-is-what-matters.
html.

18 David Edey, "The Cost of Avoiding Conversations: How
Estate Planning Can Save Your Family Heartache,"
interview by Jeremy Keil, *Retire Today* podcast,
December 18, 2024, https://keilfp.com/blogpodcast/
david-edey-estate-plan/.

19 Bill Perkins, *Die With Zero* (Mariner Books, 2020).

20 Caitlyn Moorhead, "Here's the Average Social Security
Check: Men vs. Women," Nasdaq, March 12, 2025,
https://www.gobankingrates.com/retirement/
social-security/average-social-security-check-men-women.

21 *Widowed Individuals Receiving Social Security Retirement
Benefits* (Social Security Administration, fact sheet, 2016),
https://www.ssa.gov/news/press/factsheets/ss-customer/
widowed-ret.pdf.

22 Mariacristina De Nardi et al, "Medical Spending of the US Elderly," *Fiscal Studies* 37, 3–4 (2016):717–747, https://pmc.ncbi.nlm.nih.gov/articles/PMC6680320/.

23 De Nardi et al, "Medical Spending of the US Elderly."

24 Bernadette Fernandez, *Medigap: Background and Statistics* (Library of Congress, report, 2023), https://crsreports.congress.gov/product/pdf/R/R47552.

25 "Long-Term Care," Medicare.gov, https://www.medicare.gov/coverage/long-term-care.

26 "Medicaid: Spousal Impoverishment Protection," Wisconsin Department of Health Services, last revised January 22, 2025, https://www.dhs.wisconsin.gov/medicaid/spousal-impoverishment.htm.

27 "Wisconsin Medicaid – Home and Community-Based Services Waiver Programs," Wisconsin Department of Health Services, https://www.dhs.wisconsin.gov/publications/p1/p10059.pdf.

28 Christine Benz, *How to Retire* (Harriman House, 2024).

29 Benz, *How to Retire.*

30 "Estate Tax," Internal Revenue Service, last reviewed or updated October 29, 2024, https://www.irs.gov/businesses/small-businesses-self-employed/estate-tax.

31 Joseph Johns, "Estate and Inheritance Taxes by State, 2024," Tax Foundation, November 12, 2024, https://tax-foundation.org/data/all/state/estate-inheritance-taxes/.

32 William Sharpe, "Nobel Prize-Winning Economist on How to Solve the 'Nastiest, Hardest Problem' in Retirement," *Barron's*, November 15, 2019, https://www.barrons.com/articles/william-sharpe-how-to-secure-lasting-retirement-income-51573837934.

33 Deidre McPhillips, "US Life Expectancy Has Rebounded Closer to Pre-Pandemic Levels," *CNN*, December 19, 2024, https://www.cnn.com/2024/12/19/health/us-life-expectancy-2023/index.html.

34 Sherry L. Murphy et al, "How Long Can We Expect to Live?" in *Mortality in the United States, 2023* (CDC National Center for Health Statistics data brief, 2024), https://www.cdc.gov/nchs/products/databriefs/db521.htm#section_1.

35 Wenliang Hou, "How Accurate Are Retirees' Assessments of Their Retirement Risk?" Working Paper 2020-14 (Center for Retirement Research at Boston College, July 2020), https://crr.bc.edu/wp-content/uploads/2020/07/wp_2020-14.pdf.

36 *2025 Retirement Confidence Survey* (Employee Benefit Research Institute, 2025), https://www.ebri.org/retirement/retirement-confidence-survey.

37 "Actuarial Life Table," Social Security Administration, https://www.ssa.gov/oact/STATS/table4c6.html.

38 Longevity Illustrator, https://www.longevityillustrator.org/.

39 Hou, "How Accurate Are Retirees' Assessments of Their Retirement Risk?" https://crr.bc.edu/ half-of-retirees-afraid-to-use-savings/.

40 Arna Olafsson and Michaela Pagel, "The Retirement-Consumption Puzzle: New Evidence from Personal Finances," Working Paper 24405 (National Bureau of Economic Research, March 2018), https://www.bls.gov/ cex/research_papers/pdf/the-retirement-consumption-puzzle.pdf.

41 "401(k) Participant Survey," Charles Schwab, August 2014, https://www.schwabrt.com/Content/docs/2014%20 Schwab%20401(k)%20Participant%20Survey%20Deck%20 FINAL.PDF.

42 Todd Taylor et al, "The Decumulation Paradox: Why Are Retirees Not Spending More?" *Investments & Wealth Monitor* (July/August 2018), https://www.newyorklife. com/assets/newsroom/docs/pdfs/114_The_Decumulation_ Paradox_011222.pdf.

43 Todd Taylor et al, "The Decumulation Paradox."

44 Anna Rappaport, *Insights on Spending and Asset Management in Retirement* (Society of Actuaries, 2019), https://www.soa.org/globalassets/assets/files/resources/ research-report/2019/2019-spending-asset-management-report.pdf.

45 William P. Bengen, "Determining Withdrawal Rates Using Historical Data," *Journal of Financial Planning* (October 1994, https://www.financialplanningassociation.org/

sites/default/files/2021-04/MAR04%20Determining%20
Withdrawal%20Rates%20Using%20Historical%20Data.pdf.

46 Michael Kitces, "Consumption Gap in Retirement: Why
Most Retirees Will Never Spend Down Their Portfolio,"
Nerd's Eye View, https://www.kitces.com/blog/consump-
tion-gap-in-retirement-why-most-retirees-will-never-
spend-down-their-portfolio/.

47 Richard W. Johnson, *What is the Lifetime Risk of Needing
and Receiving Long-Term Services and Supports?* (Office of
the Assistant Secretary for Planning and Evaluation, 2019),
https://aspe.hhs.gov/reports/what-lifetime-risk-needing-
receiving-long-term-services-supports-0.

48 Johnson, *Long-Term Services and Supports.*

49 Johnson, *Long-Term Services and Supports.*

50 "What's in a Retirement Number?" ING, https://www.ing.
com/Newsroom/News/Whats-in-a-retirement-number.htm.

51 Jeffrey Brown et al, *Trends in Retirement and Retirement
Income Choices by TIAA Participants: 2000–2018* (TIAA
Institute, 2021), https://www.tiaa.org/public/institute/pub-
lication/2021/trends-retirement-and-retirement-income-
choices-tiaa-participants-2000-2018.

52 Todd Taylor and Kelli Faust, *Understanding Underspending
in Retirement: The Decumulation Paradox Reexamined* (New
York Life, 2023), https://www.nylannuities.com/connect-
edassets/final-assets/marketing-materials/white-paper/
TPD_Client_Whitepaper_Decumulation_paradox.pdf.

53 *Retirement Risk Survey Series* (Society of Actuaries, 2001–2021), https://www.soa.org/research/topics/research-post-retirement-needs-and-risks/#risksurvey.

54 Sudipto Banerjee, "Expenditure Patterns of Older Americans, 2001–2009," EBRI Issue Brief, no. 368 (2012), https://papers.ssrn.com/sol3/papers.cfm?abstract_id=2007190.

55 Jane Wollman Rusoff, "Milevsky: The Most Important Financial Goal in Retirement Isn't What You Think," ThinkAdvisor, March 18, 2022, https://www.thinkadvisor.com/2022/03/18/milevsky-not-going-broke-isnt-the-most-important-financial-goal-in-retirement/.

56 Jane Wollman Rusoff, "Milevsky."

Thank You

Thank you to Nicole Gebhardt and the team at Niche Pressworks for their coaching and support throughout my book writing process.

Thank you to Emily Guy Birken for writing the foreword and serving as a shining example of great retirement planning book writing.

Thank you to the hundreds of retirees whom I've met, worked with, and presented these retirement planning concepts to. Your sharing of your dreams, and your worries, helped me refine this process so I can help you and others make better retirement decisions.

Thank you, most of all, to my family — my two daughters and especially to my wife, Robyn. Everything I do in life, this book included, would not be possible without your love and support.

Glossary

Employer stock: Shares of stock in the company where you work. When held within a 401(k), these shares may qualify for Net Unrealized Appreciation (NUA) tax treatment, allowing you to transfer the stock out of the plan under specific rules. This could allow you to pay lower long-term capital gains tax rates on the stock's appreciation rather than ordinary income tax.

In-service distribution: A withdrawal from your 401(k) while still employed. Typically available starting at age 59½, this allows you to roll over funds to an IRA without leaving your job. It could also be used to take advantage of Net Unrealized Appreciation (NUA) rules, potentially lowering taxes on employer stock.

Lump-sum pension option: An option to receive a one-time payment from your pension instead of guaranteed lifetime monthly payments. Pensions typically provide guaranteed monthly income starting at your normal retirement age, but many plans allow you to take a lump sum instead. The lump-sum amount is calculated by plan actuaries based on interest rates and life expectancy, which means the value is not based on a formula like your normal retirement age pension amount but instead fluctuates up and down based on economic conditions.

Net Unrealized Appreciation (NUA): A little-known tax rule that allows you to transfer employer stock from your 401(k), following plan rules, and potentially change the tax treatment of its growth. Instead of paying ordinary income tax on the stock's growth, you may qualify for lower long-term capital gains tax rates on the unrealized gains.

Present value: The amount of money needed today to produce a series of future cash flows based on current interest rates and a specific time frame. In pensions, an exact length of time is not used, but is instead determined by the probability of a retiree living long enough to receive each future payment, using mortality tables to estimate life expectancy.

Required minimum distributions (RMDs): Mandatory withdrawals from traditional retirement accounts. You will pay a tax penalty if you do not take your RMDs on time.

Social Security level/accelerated pension option: If you retire before age 62, this pension option provides higher monthly payments until age 62, when it is permanently reduced by the estimated amount of your age 62 Social Security benefit. This shifts more pension income to the early years of retirement but results in a lower lifetime pension payment if you live longer than expected. Because of the drop in guaranteed monthly income at 62 from this option, many retirees feel pressured to claim Social Security early, at a 30 percent reduction from their full retirement age amount, even if it is not the best financial decision for them. This option is more common in government pension plans than in corporate pension plans.

Summary Plan Description (SPD): A document summarizing the key details of your benefit plan, such as your 401(k) or pension. It outlines important rules, including when and how you can access funds, how you earn pension benefits, and how starting your pension early may affect your payments.

Volatility: A measure of risk based on the frequency and level of the ups and downs you see in your investments. Most people are more concerned about the downside risk of losing money versus the upside risk of gaining more than expected.

About Jeremy Keil

Jeremy Keil, CFP®, CFA®, is the retirement planner you turn to when you're ready to retire but don't know how to do it. He's a retirement-focused financial advisor, the host of the *Retire Today* podcast, and the face behind the *Mr. Retirement* YouTube channel.

For over two decades, Jeremy has helped hundreds of people retire with confidence using his signature Retirement Master Plan — a simple process designed to help you make more income, pay less in taxes, and avoid big retirement mistakes.

Growing up, Jeremy loved solving math and logic puzzles. When he became a financial advisor, he realized retirement planning was just a bigger, more important puzzle — helping you piece together your finances to create a better, more secure retirement.

While serving as an adjunct professor at Concordia University Wisconsin and Wisconsin Lutheran College, Jeremy developed a gift for turning complex financial topics into clear, practical lessons.

Whether in the classroom, delivering educational seminars, or in client meetings, his focus has always been the same: to help you know more about your money so you will feel better about your money and make better money decisions.

When he's not solving retirement puzzles, you'll find Jeremy with his wife, Robyn, and their two daughters — likely at a swim meet, soccer game, basketball court, or hanging out with their church family at Lakepoint in Muskego, Wisconsin.

Want to learn more about how Jeremy and his team can help you solve your retirement puzzle? Head over to JeremyKeil.com.

CONTACT

Website: JeremyKeil.com
LinkedIn: LinkedIn.com/in/MrRetirement/
YouTube: YouTube.com/@MrRetirement

www.ingramcontent.com/pod-product-compliance
Lightning Source LLC
Chambersburg PA
CBHW071555210326
41597CB00019B/3256